THE
ARAPAHO

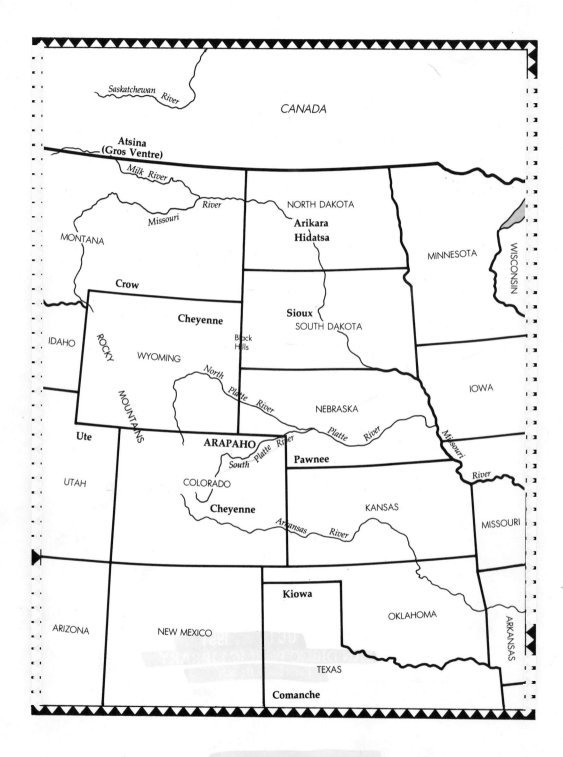

THE ARAPAHO

Loretta Fowler
City University of New York

Frank W. Porter III
General Editor

CHELSEA HOUSE PUBLISHERS
New York   Philadelphia

On the cover Peyote fan made in the late 19th century.

Chelsea House Publishers
Editor-in-Chief Nancy Toff
Executive Editor Remmel T. Nunn
Managing Editor Karyn Gullen Browne
Copy Chief Juliann Barbato
Picture Editor Adrian G. Allen
Art Director Maria Epes
Manufacturing Manager Gerald Levine

Indians of North America
Senior Editor Marjorie P. K. Weiser

Staff for **THE ARAPAHO**
Associate Editor Clifford W. Crouch
Copy Editor Lisa S. Fenev
Deputy Copy Chief Ellen Scordato
Editorial Assistant Claire Wilson
Assistant Art Director Loraine Machlin
Designer Donna Sinisgalli
Designer Assistant James Baker
Picture Researcher Alan Gottlieb
Production Coordinator Joseph Romano

3 5 7 9 8 6 4 2

Library of Congress Cataloging-in-Publication Data

Fowler, Loretta, 1944–
The Arapaho / Loretta Fowler.
p. cm.—(Indians of North America)
Bibliography: p.
Includes index.
Summary: Examines the culture, history, and changing
fortunes of the Arapaho Indians.
ISBN 1-55546-690-7.
    0-7910-0371-X (pbk.)
1. Arapaho Indians—Juvenile Literature. [1. Arapaho
Indians. 2. Indians of North America.] I. Title. II. Series:
Indians of North America (Chelsea House Publishers)
E99.A7F677 1989   88-33988
973'.0497—dc19   CIP
                                         AC

CONTENTS

INDIANS OF NORTH AMERICA

The Abenaki

American Indian
   Literature

The Apache

The Arapaho

The Archaeology
   of North America

The Aztecs

The Cahuilla

The Catawbas

The Cherokee

The Cheyenne

The Chickasaw

The Chinook

The Chipewyan

The Choctaw

The Chumash

The Coast Salish Peoples

The Comanche

The Creeks

The Crow

The Eskimo

Federal Indian Policy

The Hidatsa

The Huron

The Iroquois

The Kiowa

The Kwakiutl

The Lenapes

The Lumbee

The Maya

The Menominee

The Modoc

The Montagnais-Naskapi

The Nanticoke

The Narragansett

The Navajo

The Nez Perce

The Ojibwa

The Osage

The Paiute

The Pima-Maricopa

The Potawatomi

The Powhatan Tribes

The Pueblo

The Quapaw

The Seminole

The Tarahumara

The Tunica-Biloxi

Urban Indians

The Wampanoag

Women in American
   Indian Society

The Yakima

The Yankton Sioux

The Yuma

CHELSEA HOUSE PUBLISHERS

INDIANS OF NORTH AMERICA: CONFLICT AND SURVIVAL

Frank W. Porter III

The Indians survived our open intention of wiping them out, and since the tide turned they have even weathered our good intentions toward them, which can be much more deadly.

John Steinbeck
America and Americans

When Europeans first reached the North American continent, they found hundreds of tribes occupying a vast and rich country. The newcomers quickly recognized the wealth of natural resources. They were not, however, so quick or willing to recognize the spiritual, cultural, and intellectual riches of the people they called Indians.

The Indians of North America examines the problems that develop when people with different cultures come together. For American Indians, the consequences of their interaction with non-Indian people have been both productive and tragic. The Europeans believed they had "discovered" a "New World," but their religious bigotry, cultural bias, and materialistic world view kept them from appreciating and understanding the people who lived in it. All too often they attempted to change the way of life of the indigenous people. The Spanish conquistadores wanted the Indians as a source of labor. The Christian missionaries, many of whom were English, viewed them as potential converts. French traders and trappers used the Indians as a means to obtain pelts. As Francis Parkman, the 19th-century historian, stated, "Spanish civilization crushed the Indian; English civilization scorned and neglected him; French civilization embraced and cherished him."

7

Nearly 500 years later, many people think of American Indians as curious vestiges of a distant past, waging a futile war to survive in a Space Age society. Even today, our understanding of the history and culture of American Indians is too often derived from unsympathetic, culturally biased, and inaccurate reports. The American Indian, described and portrayed in thousands of movies, television programs, books, articles, and government studies, has either been raised to the status of the "noble savage" or disparaged as the "wild Indian" who resisted the westward expansion of the American frontier.

Where in this popular view are the real Indians, the human beings and communities whose ancestors can be traced back to ice-age hunters? Where are the creative and indomitable people whose sophisticated technologies used the natural resources to ensure their survival, whose military skill might even have prevented European settlement of North America if not for devastating epidemics and disruption of the ecology? Where are the men and women who are today diligently struggling to assert their legal rights and express once again the value of their heritage?

The various Indian tribes of North America, like people everywhere, have a history that includes population expansion, adaptation to a range of regional environments, trade across wide networks, internal strife, and warfare. This was the reality. Europeans justified their conquests, however, by creating a mythical image of the New World and its native people. In this myth, the New World was a virgin land, waiting for the Europeans. The arrival of Christopher Columbus ended a timeless primitiveness for the original inhabitants.

Also part of this myth was the debate over the origins of the American Indians. Fantastic and diverse answers were proposed by the early explorers, missionaries, and settlers. Some thought that the Indians were descended from the Ten Lost Tribes of Israel, others that they were descended from inhabitants of the lost continent of Atlantis. One writer suggested that the Indians had reached North America in another Noah's ark.

A later myth, perpetrated by many historians, focused on the relentless persecution during the past five centuries until only a scattering of these "primitive" people remained to be herded onto reservations. This view fails to chronicle the overt and covert ways in which the Indians successfully coped with the intruders.

All of these myths presented one-sided interpretations that ignored the complexity of European and American events and policies. All left serious questions unanswered. What were the origins of the American Indians? Where did they come from? How and when did they get to the New World? What was their life—their culture—really like?

In the late 1800s, anthropologists and archaeologists in the Smithsonian Institution's newly created Bureau of American Ethnology in Washington,

D.C., began to study scientifically the history and culture of the Indians of North America. They were motivated by an honest belief that the Indians were on the verge of extinction and that along with them would vanish their languages, religious beliefs, technology, myths, and legends. These men and women went out to visit, study, and record data from as many Indian communities as possible before this information was forever lost.

By this time there was a new myth in the national consciousness. American Indians existed as figures in the American past. They had performed a historical mission. They had challenged white settlers who trekked across the continent. Once conquered, however, they were supposed to accept graciously the way of life of their conquerors.

The reality again was different. American Indians resisted both actively and passively. They refused to lose their unique identity, to be assimilated into white society. Many whites viewed the Indians not only as members of a conquered nation but also as "inferior" and "unequal." The rights of the Indians could be expanded, contracted, or modified as the conquerors saw fit. In every generation, white society asked itself what to do with the American Indians. Their answers have resulted in the twists and turns of federal Indian policy.

There were two general approaches. One way was to raise the Indians to a "higher level" by "civilizing" them. Zealous missionaries considered it their Christian duty to elevate the Indian through conversion and scanty education. The other approach was to ignore the Indians until they disappeared under pressure from the ever-expanding white society. The myth of the "vanishing Indian" gave stronger support to the latter option, helping to justify the taking of the Indians' land.

Prior to the end of the 18th century, there was no national policy on Indians simply because the American nation has not yet come into existence. American Indians similarly did not possess a political or social unity with which to confront the various Europeans. They were not homogeneous. Rather, they were loosely formed bands and tribes, speaking nearly 300 languages and thousands of dialects. The collective identity felt by Indians today is a result of their common experiences of defeat and/or mistreatment at the hands of whites.

During the colonial period, the British crown did not have a coordinated policy toward the Indians of North America. Specific tribes (most notably the Iroquois and the Cherokee) became military and political pawns used by both the crown and the individual colonies. The success of the American Revolution brought no immediate change. When the United States acquired new territory from France and Mexico in the early 19th century, the federal government wanted to open this land to settlement by homesteaders. But the Indian tribes that lived on this land had signed treaties with European governments assuring their title to the land. Now the United States assumed legal responsibility for honoring these treaties.

At first, President Thomas Jefferson believed that the Louisiana Purchase contained sufficient land for both the Indians and the white population. Within a generation, though, it became clear that the Indians would not be allowed to remain. In the 1830s the federal government began to coerce the eastern tribes to sign treaties agreeing to relinquish their ancestral land and move west of the Mississippi River. Whenever these negotiations failed, President Andrew Jackson used the military to remove the Indians. The southeastern tribes, promised food and transportation during their removal to the West, were instead forced to walk the "Trail of Tears." More than 4,000 men, woman, and children died during this forced march. The "removal policy" was successful in opening the land to homesteaders, but it created enormous hardships for the Indians.

By 1871 most of the tribes in the United States had signed treaties ceding most or all of their ancestral land in exchange for reservations and welfare. The treaty terms were intended to bind both parties for all time. But in the General Allotment Act of 1887, the federal government changed its policy again. Now the goal was to make tribal members into individual landowners and farmers, encouraging their absorption into white society. This policy was advantageous to whites who were eager to acquire Indian land, but it proved disastrous for the Indians. One hundred thirty-eight million acres of reservation land were subdivided into tracts of 160, 80, or as little as 40 acres, and allotted tribe members on an individual basis. Land owned in this way was said to have "trust status" and could not be sold. But the surplus land—all Indian land not allotted to individuals—was opened (for sale) to white settlers. Ultimately, more than 90 million acres of land were taken from the Indians by legal and illegal means.

The resulting loss of land was a catastrophe for the Indians. It was necessary to make it illegal for Indians to sell their land to non-Indians. The Indian Reorganization Act of 1934 officially ended the allotment period. Tribes that voted to accept the provisions of this act were reorganized, and an effort was made to purchase land within preexisting reservations to restore an adequate land base.

Ten years later, in 1944, federal Indian policy again shifted. Now the federal government wanted to get out of the "Indian business." In 1953 an act of Congress named specific tribes whose trust status was to be ended "at the earliest possible time." This new law enabled the United States to end unilaterally, whether the Indians wished it or not, the special status that protected the land in Indian tribal reservations. In the 1950s federal Indian policy was to transfer federal responsibility and jurisdiction to state governments, encourage the physical relocation of Indian peoples from reservations to urban areas, and hasten the termination, or extinction, of tribes.

Between 1954 and 1962 Congress passed specific laws authorizing the termination of more than 100 tribal groups. The stated purpose of the termination policy was to ensure the full and complete integration of Indians into American society. However, there is a less benign way to interpret this legislation. Even as termination was being discussed in Congress, 133 separate bills were introduced to permit the transfer of trust land ownership from Indians to non-Indians.

With the Johnson administration in the 1960s the federal government began to reject termination. In the 1970s yet another Indian policy emerged. Known as "self-determination," it favored keeping the protective role of the federal government while increasing tribal participation in, and control of, important areas of local government. In 1983 President Reagan, in a policy statement on Indian affairs, restated the unique "government is government" relationship of the United States with the Indians. However, federal programs since then have moved toward transferring Indian affairs to individual states, which have long desired to gain control of Indian land and resources.

As long as American Indians retain power, land, and resources that are coveted by the states and the federal government, there will continue to be a "clash of cultures," and the issues will be contested in the courts, Congress, the White House, and even in the international human rights community. To give all Americans a greater comprehension of the issues and conflicts involving American Indians today is a major goal of this series. These issues are not easily understood, nor can these conflicts be readily resolved. The study of North American Indian history and culture is a necessary and important step toward that comprehension. All Americans must learn the history of the relations between the Indians and the federal government, recognize the unique legal status of the Indians, and understand the heritage and cultures of the Indians of North America.

A Smoke—Arapaho, *photographed by Edward S. Curtis in 1910.*
The pipe shown here is a social, rather than sacred, one, but a tribal
elder, by virtue of his position, could also use it to transmit prayers.

DEVOTEES
AND
PROPHETS

In the beginning, according to Arapaho accounts, the First Pipe Keeper floated on a limitless body of water with the Flat Pipe. He fasted and prayed to the Creator, who inspired him to send the duck to search beneath the water's surface. The duck emerged with a little bit of dirt, which the First Pipe Keeper put on the Pipe. Then he sent the turtle to the bottom, and it, too, returned with dirt. The First Pipe Keeper put this dirt on the Pipe and blew it all off toward each of the four directions. In doing so, he created the earth. Then he made the sun and moon, man and woman, and vegetable and animal life, followed by day and night and the four seasons. He then taught the first people the religious rites that they would need. The duck and turtle were placed with the Pipe into a bundle, and the Arapaho—descendants of that first man and woman—have been responsible for them ever since. For the Arapaho the contents of the bundle are symbols of the creation, and their custody of the bundle a sacred trust.

The Arapaho believed that supernatural power, and the life force itself, emanated from the Creator, or from the "Great Mystery Above." During mythological times, the Creator infused this power into other beings—forces of nature, animals, and some minerals. The Arapaho could appeal to these supernatural beings for help. The Creator's power on earth was first and foremost manifest in the Flat Pipe. The sacred bundle from the creation story was a medium through which prayers were conveyed to the Creator.

James Mooney, an ethnologist with the Smithsonian Institution, in Washington, D.C., wrote in 1890 that the Arapaho were an intensely religious people, "devotees and prophets, continuously seeing signs and wonders." The Arapaho believed that religious devotion would be rewarded with help from the Creator in achieving health, happiness, and success. If they gave the Creator proper respect, prayer, and supplication, then cosmic, natural, and social forces would operate harmoniously. Elderly people had primary responsibility for maintaining good relations with the Creator, and people sought their assistance in petitioning for supernatural aid.

All adults exerted much effort in communicating with the Creator through prayer, or earnest "wish-thought." They prayed often, using pipes, smoke, steam, or song to convey their prayers to the Creator above. Sacrifice, in the form of offerings, was believed to express the supplicant's sincerity and frequently accompanied prayer. Offerings might include food (often presented as gifts to elders), tobacco or a filled pipe, property, or even the sacrifice of a finger joint or a bit of flesh.

The Arapaho's accounts of their past credit heroes with showing the people how to thrive in the world. Through supernatural aid these heroes made important discoveries and performed extraordinary deeds. One hero taught the Arapaho how to make an enclosure near a cliff to trap buffalo, and how to catch and train horses. Another discovered how to make and use bone tools: the first arrowhead (from the rib of a buffalo) and the first bow—both technological advances that made hunting easier—and how to use stone to shape a knife made from the shoulder blade of a buffalo. A third invented a more efficient way of making fire by striking flint rather than using a drill. The Arapaho's major ceremonies were also believed to have originated in individuals' encounters with supernatural beings.

In the 1840s, the Arapaho were well known to pioneers crossing the Great Plains, but when—and from where—the Arapaho moved into the area is still uncertain. They were probably living on the northern Plains west of the Missouri River before the 18th century. No record exists that shows any explorers or traders who encountered them east of the Missouri, so their migration westward must have occurred before the arrival of these European adventurers in the late 17th and early 18th centuries. The Arapaho language belongs to the Algonquian family. Because tribes speaking other languages from this group lived from the Atlantic coastline westward to the Great Lakes area, it seems likely that the Arapaho once lived northeast of the Missouri River and then moved westward onto the Plains.

Archaeologists have not been able to conclusively identify any ancient site or artifact as belonging to the Arapaho. Their oral traditions, however, indicate that they once hunted buffalo on foot. Until about 1730 they probably relied on dogs to help transport their belongings as they followed the immense buffalo herds, moving according to the animals' seasonal migration patterns. Their possessions were often transported on a *travois*, an A-shaped platform whose back end dragged along the ground as it was pulled by a harnessed dog.

Shortly after 1730 the Arapaho seem to have acquired horses by trading with, or raiding, tribes to the south.

A travois being pulled by a horse to transport belongings. Before the Indians had horses, they attached travois to dogs. A woman carries her child on the travois in this 1908 photograph by Edward S. Curtis taken among the Atsina, or Gros Ventre, a tribe closely related to the Arapaho.

These people in turn had gotten their horses by raiding Spanish settlements in what is now New Mexico and Texas. The introduction of the horse radically changed the Arapaho's lives. In past years, the Arapaho had driven the buffalo over cliffs or into enclosures, then killed the trapped animals with arrows and spears tipped with stone points, and butchered them with blades of stone or bone. Now hunters mounted on horseback could race alongside the buffalo, killing more efficiently than they had been able to do on foot. The horse also expanded the Arapaho's ability to trade products of the hunt, as well as horses, with other tribes.

They had an active trade relationship with the farming villages of the Arikara, Mandan, and Hidatsa on the Missouri River, exchanging their surplus meat and hides for the villagers' extra beans, corn, and squash. The Arikara called the Arapaho "Colored Stone Village [People]," possibly because gemstones from the Southwest were among the items the Arapaho traded. The Hidatsa called them "Bison-Path Indians."

The Arapaho probably acquired not only corn and other agricultural products from these neighboring tribes but new ceremonies as well. The elaborate men's society rituals, and probably other elements of late 18th- and 19th-century Arapaho religious life, may have been adapted from or influenced by contacts with these villagers. It was at a trade fair (a gathering of Indian traders and sometimes non-Indian traders as well) in 1795, in the Black Hills of what is now South Dakota, that Arapaho bands from the central and southern plains encountered the trader-explorer Jean Baptiste Trudeau. He left the first written account of the Arapaho. Others would follow.

The northern bands of Arapaho, known as the Atsina or Gros Ventre ("Big Bellies"), met English traders in the mid-18th century in the upper Saskatchewan River country of Canada. The Atsina were eventually pushed south into Montana by other tribes and by the mid-19th century were living between the Missouri and Milk rivers. In 1878 they settled on a reservation in

Long's Peak in Estes Park, *an oil painting by Albert Bierstadt (1830–1902). This area of central Colorado, known as The Parks, is where the Arapaho moved after they were forced out of the Black Hills by the Cheyenne and Sioux.*

northern Montana, and their history took a course different from that of either the Northern or Southern Arapaho, who are the subjects of this book.

In the late 18th century, Arapaho bands on the central and southern Plains ranged from what is now southeastern Montana and eastern Wyoming south to the headwaters of the Platte River. Pressed by the Cheyenne and then by hostile Sioux tribes, who had taken control of the Black Hills area, they began to move southwest. By the early 19th century the Arapaho controlled the area known as the Parks and adjacent Plains in what is now west-central Colorado and were warring with several neighboring tribes there: the Ute to the west, the Crow north of the Platte River, and the Pawnee to the east. They were also making more frequent raids on the Kiowa and Comanche to the south in order to increase their supply of horses.

About 1820 the Arapaho began to form an alliance with the Cheyenne to fight the Sioux north of the Platte and the Kiowa and Comanche to the south. The two allies pushed the Kiowa and Comanche south of the Arkansas River and gradually came to dominate the area between the Platte and Arkansas rivers as far as present-day eastern Colorado.

In the early 19th century the Arapaho frequently came in contact with American fur trappers in the foothills of the Rocky Mountains and near the headwaters of the Platte and Arkansas rivers. The traders referred to them by the Crow Indians' name for the tribe, "Alappahó," which meant "People with Many Tattoos." (Arapaho men commonly had three small circles tattooed horizontally across their chests. Women had a single circle tattooed upon their foreheads. The tattoos were made by pricking the skin with cactus spines and rubbing powdered charcoal into the wound. This left a sky-blue mark after healing.) The traders' pronunciation of this name led to the widespread use of the name Arapaho.

The Arapaho sometimes raided trade caravans traveling to and from the Spanish settlements, but they also traded peacefully with several Americans. These included the brothers William and Charles Bent, who built posts in Arapaho country in the early 1830s. During the first half of the century, the Arapaho continued to hunt. At the same time they began to incorporate into their tool kits and decorative arts manufactured goods, such as knives and beads, that they acquired from traders.

The Arapaho would become well known to these traders and to the pioneers who crossed the western Plains on their way to settle in Oregon and California after 1840. This flood of emigrants would soon ravage the Arapaho's hunting grounds, and the tribe would become increasingly dependent on traders for sustenance as well as luxury items. Later in the 19th century the U.S. Army would find the Arapaho to be deadly adversaries. Yet, for the most part, the tribe's leaders strove to follow a course of peaceful coexistence with this new and overwhelming civilization. Over many years, traders, military and government officials, missionaries, journalists, and anthropologists would write about these and other aspects of Arapaho life, as the tribe attempted to defend itself against the onslaught of U.S. expansion.

But until the great disruptions of the 1840s and later, the Arapaho were able to obtain all the necessities of life by hunting big game and gathering roots and berries that existed wild on the prairie. Flat Pipe rituals were held at the start of every spring and fall to ensure the renewal of these seasonal resources. In the spring the buffalo began to move about in small herds. Arapaho family groups that had been scattered during the winter in the sheltered Rocky Mountain foothills joined forces so the men could hunt buffalo together. Mounted on horses, the men chased the herds. Sometimes they singled out the animals they wanted and cut them off from the rest of the herd in order to kill them more easily. When there were enough men, they would surround the herd and close it in, repeatedly shooting arrows into it until several animals were killed or seriously wounded. Allowing the surviving buffalo to escape, the hunters could finish off those whose wounds forced them to lag behind. Arapaho bows were made of wood—often cedar—supported by layers of sinew (animal tendon) to add flexibility and strength. The arrow points were of flint. (Later these were gradually replaced with metal ones as the Arapaho came to trade regularly with the Mexicans and Americans.)

The men butchered the game before bringing it back to camp. They used knives made either of flint or from the shoulder blade of a buffalo. (Later they would use metal knives obtained in trade.) After butchering, the meat was transported to camp on the backs of packhorses to be smoked and dried. The women in each family cooked and preserved the meat the hunters brought back and prepared the hides for use as clothing and as tipi covers. In the summer and early fall, when the buffalo herds were largest, the bands regularly came together. They pitched their tipis in a circle. Ceremonies were held in the center of the camp circle, after which groups of men went out to hunt or to raid other tribes, while women worked to dry enough meat, roots, and berries for the winter months.

In winter the large camps were dissolved again. Each band, composed of 20 to 80 families, moved to its favorite winter campsite in the sheltered, wooded areas along the mountain streams. During this season, the men

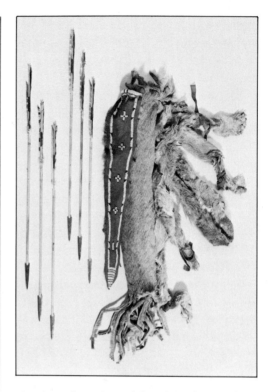

An Arapaho quiver of deerskin, decorated with five-bead stitchwork, and arrows.

hunted for deer and small game. They wore snowshoes made of thongs or narrow strips of rawhide forming a net that was fastened to a wooden frame. It was common for a man to use a wood or bone whistle to lure a deer; hunters were expert at imitating the sounds of various animals.

Throughout the year, women's work was as valued as the men's hunting duties. Their work was hard, but women did not consider it drudgery. They were responsible for setting up and moving camp, collecting firewood and edible plants, cooking, and making the family's clothing and shelter. The preparation of animal hides occupied much of the women's time. Rawhide was made by scraping the flesh and hair from a hide, then stretching the skin on the ground, where it was held in position with pegs and left to dry until stiff. Deer or elk skins were used for shirts, dresses, moccasins, and leggings. The skins were soaked, scraped, softened, stretched, and tanned. Then they were cut into the desired pattern and sewn together with sinew pulled through holes punched with an awl.

Women wore dresses that hung almost to the ankle, moccasins with attached leggings that reached the knee and were tied with garters, and, in winter, blankets. Men wore buckskin shirts, leggings that covered their legs from ankle to hip, breechcloths, moccasins, and, in winter, robes of buffalo skin. Buffalo hides were thicker than those of deer and elk and were therefore used for robes as well as tipi covers. Buffalo hair was thickest in the fall, so that is when the women made the unscraped winter robes. Scraped buffalo skins were used for tipi covers.

A family consisted of a man and his wife or wives (the Arapaho were polygynous), their children, and perhaps other relatives such as a husband's younger brother or a spouse's widowed parent. Each family had its own tipi. Some tipis were larger than others and had more and better furnishings. These belonged to those men who were wealthiest in horses. They could use more horses to drag extra poles, could

accumulate more hides, and could also afford more than one wife. They could lend horses to others, who were then obligated to support their claims to leadership and status. Horse owners received part of the kill and with this surplus could entertain, pay the expenses of ceremonies, and attract followers.

To make a tipi, a foundation of poles was set into the ground. Over it was stretched a covering made of 15 to 20 buffalo skins sewn together. The base of this cover was secured to the ground with stones or pegs. In winter the outside of the cover was banked with three feet of earth to retain warmth. The tipi

A scraper made of antler, used to remove hair, fat, and other tissue from animal hides.

was lined inside, and on this lining were painted pictures of the husband's war exploits.

In the center of the tipi was a fire, which was created by friction from twirling a drill or striking two stones together over tinder. Wood or dried buffalo dung provided the fuel that kept the fire burning. The chief furnishing of the tipi was a foot-high platform that served as both bed and sofa. It was made of poles and rested on the hard-packed dirt floor (wealthier families sometimes covered the floor with buffalo skins). The platform was covered with a woven mat of willow rods that had one end upraised. Covered with hides for warmth and softness, the bed also served as a couch by day. Pillows were made of buckskin stuffed with buffalo hair.

Food was eaten while seated on a piece of rawhide placed on the floor of the tipi. Small pieces of rawhide served as plates, and there were wooden bowls and spoons made of horn. There were no regularly scheduled mealtimes. People ate when they were hungry or when a hunter returned with meat. A meal might consist of dried meat or

An Arapaho camp, photographed in the early 1870s. The tipi is made of sewn buffalo skins with door flaps of hairy, unscraped hide. In the background, a hide hangs over a meat-curing rack to dry.

pemmican (a mixture of dried meat and berries, blended with tallow). Berries, picked by women in summer, were used in several ways: eaten fresh or dried or made into soup. Tea made from herbs such as mint was a favorite beverage. Most dishes were a kind of stew made from meat and wild roots, such as turnips or potatoes. These foods were cut up and put into a rawhide container into which water had been brought to a boil by dropping red-hot stones into the liquid. By the middle of the 19th century, however, most families cooked in a metal pot obtained in trade.

Because the Arapaho were on the move much of the time, containers of all sorts were important to the household, and all were made by the women. From buffalo bladders they made bags for carrying water. After the women made camp, water was stored in baskets made of plant fiber and coated with pitch. Women made many types of soft-skin bags for their personal use: pouches to hold quills and paints; sheathes for knives and awls; toilet pouches for face paints, earrings, bracelets, hair parters, and porcupine-tail hairbrushes; bags for sewing gear. They made large soft-skin bags to carry the household's clothing. They made firmer bags of untanned rawhide, called parfleches, which were made in many sizes and used to transport household articles and foodstuffs.

The women painted designs on the stiff rawhide parfleches and embroidered the soft-skin bags. Women also embroidered designs on buckskin tipi ornaments, clothing, and other household objects, incorporating either dyed porcupine quills or, by the mid-19th century, glass beads obtained from traders. Their designs expressed prayers or instructions received in dreams. These designs on robes, cradles, and tipi ornaments were created by women who were considered authorities on ritual matters.

Ritual, prayer, sacrifice, and other signs of religious devotion permeated all aspects of Arapaho life. The Arapaho's decorative art was shaped by prayers and visions; their quest for subsistence was guided by ceremonial acts. From birth to death, concern about relating to the Creator shaped every Arapaho's everyday life. No wonder, then, that the Arapaho, more than any other Plains people he visited, impressed anthropologist James Mooney as "devotees and prophets." ▲

A Southern Arapaho baby in a cloth cradle. By the late 19th century deerskin was no longer available to make cradles or other items because game had been overhunted and had become increasingly scarce.

THE FOUR HILLS
OF LIFE

All Arapaho traveled through four stages, or "hills of life"—childhood, youth, adulthood, and old age. The duties, responsibilities, and privileges of males and females changed at each stage. The Arapaho symbolically equated the life cycle with the movement of the sun, the four cardinal directions, and the progress of the seasons. They believed, too, that an individual could be reborn after death. A child born with wrinkles or scars and dents, for example, might be the reincarnation of an elder or someone who had suffered wounds in a previous life.

The Arapaho believed that humans were endowed by the Creator with the ability to think and that thought itself could cause things to happen. Speaking of prenatal life or birth, for example, could cause pregnancy, and people with exceptional powers of thought could cause sterility. If a pregnant woman were startled or badly frightened, the impression left in her mind could cause her child to have birth defects or marks.

Immediately after birth, a baby was rubbed with red paint made of red earth mixed with tallow. The paint symbol-

ized prayers for strength and health. Then the baby was placed inside a cradle made of ornamented buckskin stretched over a willow frame. Dried and finely ground buffalo manure was packed inside the cradle to absorb body wastes and prevent chafing. While the mother worked she leaned the cradle against a tree, and when she traveled on horseback she attached it to her saddle horn.

When infants were taken out of their cradles, they were wrapped in the tanned hide of an unborn buffalo, with its soft, warm, hairy side against the baby's body. In cold weather, the baby might be put into a bag made from the skin of a wildcat. The baby's head was fitted into the head of the skin and its arms and legs placed into the skin's legs. A baby starting to crawl would be dressed in a tanned deer-hide shirt, and at the toddling stage in adult-style clothing.

Parents took special precautions to protect their children. They arranged for elders to pray on the child's behalf. Because negative wish-thoughts might come true, people refrained from talking about sickness. Symbols of positive

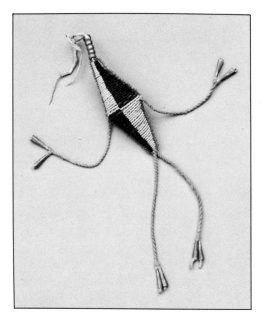

A case containing an infant's cut umbilical cord. Used as an amulet, it is decorated with beaded designs symbolizing a prayer that the child have a long, healthy, and fruitful life.

began to walk, it was attached to his or her clothing.

The child was named by an elder soon after birth. Often the child's parents would invite several elders to a feast at which the name was given, and the elders would pray for the child. A name might be derived from a brave or charitable deed. For example, an old warrior who had been the first to kill an enemy in a particular battle might name a child First Killer. Or a name might come from an extraordinary event or an unusual occurrence in nature—Yellow Bear or White Hawk, for example. An elder might also name a child after something seen in a dream or vision and regarded as a good omen. Elders' prayers were regarded as particularly beneficial because the Creator had blessed elders by allowing them to live long. Thus, if an elder gave a child his or her name, that name was believed to assure good health and a long life for its new recipient as well. Conversely, the name of a child who became ill would often be changed.

To mark special events in the development of a child—when the child first walked or spoke, for example— parents would invite tribal elders to a feast. When a small boy killed his first animal, his parents would invite elders to a feast, announce his feat, and give gifts to the guests in his honor. On all these occasions, the elders would pray for the child.

Parents also arranged for their child's ears to be pierced by a respected old warrior or an old woman who had

wish-thoughts decorated the objects surrounding the child. The baby's cradle was decorated with quillwork designs that represented the maker's prayer for the child to have a long and successful life. Only older women who had the ritual authority to do so could create these designs. At birth, the infant's umbilical cord was cut. It was then put into a beaded case, whose shape represented growth and whose design symbolized the maker's prayer that the child have a long, healthy, and productive life. The case containing the umbilical cord was attached first to the infant's cradle. Later, when the child "pierced" an enemy. Both boys and girls had their ears pierced, usually between the ages of two and five. An awl or a knife was used. The awl symbolized a spear; the hole, the enemy's wound; and the ear ornaments, dripping blood. During the piercing a war song was sung, the piercer told the story of how he had wounded an enemy, and then the piercer "charged" at the child's ear as he had charged at the

A Southern Arapaho child. Parents gave a feast for the tribal elders when a young boy or girl first learned to walk.

enemy. The child's ears could also be pierced during an important religious ceremony such as the Sun Dance. In this case it would be done by an elderly priest, or director, of the ceremony. The piercing here symbolized being struck by lightning—so the child was thereafter protected against enemy arrows. The child's crying was regarded as a sign that hardship and pain, having been endured in the piercing, would not prevent the child from growing up. The ear-piercing ceremony was, in effect, another prayer for a long and successful life.

Children learned adult tasks in play activity, in playing house and in games of skill and chance. In play they imitated the activities of their elders. The girls played with toys such as miniature saddlebags, little spoons made of horn, and tipis that were two to three feet high and held beds made with squirrel skins instead of buffalo hides. They also played with dolls made of stuffed buckskin. The dolls were sexless—clothed only in a nondescript buckskin or cloth blanket—and did not represent babies, for speaking of babies was believed to cause pregnancy. Little boys would pretend to hunt for little girls (who pretended to be their mothers) and go to war using horses and enemies made from clay.

Physical activities and sports became more important as a child grew. Children were given ponies and began to ride when they were about three years old. They also became good swimmers, playing games in the creeks

A model of a cradle containing a doll, made of beaded hide. Children took part in games and activities not only for play but also to learn adult skills and tasks.

and rivers. They might challenge one another as to who could swim underwater the farthest and longest; or they might attempt swimming across a river on their backs, with one foot sticking out of the water and a ball of mud impaled on the big toe. Boys competed against one another in shooting arrows, tossing hoops, throwing a javelin, spinning tops, and sliding sticks across the

ice. Girls played dice and stick darts and juggled a hair-stuffed buckskin ball on a string, on the foot, or from arm to palm.

Sometimes parents invited an elder who had made a success of his or her life to eat with the family, recount his or her experiences, and advise the child. Grandparents also told the children stories at night—tales of Trickster, or Spider, the wonder-worker. These stories conveyed the values by which the Arapaho lived, for Trickster was always undone by his foolish behavior.

When boys and girls reached about 12 years of age, their training for adult life began in earnest. Boys and girls were separated from one another, and even brothers and sisters now had to avoid talking to one another or even being in the other's presence.

Unlike some other tribes, the Arapaho held no ceremony for a girl when she had her first menstrual period, nor was she isolated in a special tipi. Because menstruation was believed tinged with a supernatural power that might harm others in certain circumstances, however, the girls stayed apart from the rest of the tribe. They kept company mostly with old women and avoided sacred ceremonies. After puberty there were restrictions on a young woman's freedom. She might wear a blanket to conceal her figure, and her dresses were now long sleeved and hung almost to the ankle, like those of older women. She would often live with a grandmother or other elderly female relative, who would teach her how to prepare food, tan skins, and make clothing.

Young girls and adult women spent considerable time on their appearance. In the early part of the century, women wore their hair loose and painted it. Later, they parted the hair from forehead to nape and made two braids from behind the ear. They used sweet-smelling leaves and seeds to perfume their clothing and hair. The face was painted daily to protect it from the elements.

Teenage boys, meanwhile, were instructed by older male relatives on how to hunt, make a living, and develop those social traits the Arapaho admired. In their early teens they were encouraged to participate in the Kit Fox ceremony. The Kit Fox was the first of the societies that Arapaho boys and men belonged to in the course of their lives. Young teenage boys would band together and persuade a man about 10 years older to act as their adviser. Under his tutelage they prepared for the ceremony by learning the Kit Fox dance and songs. After completing the ceremony they were bound together, obligated to assist and support one another for the rest of their lives. As Kit Foxes they trained together for adult life, racing on foot and horseback, wrestling, engaging in mock battles, and raiding households to steal meat from drying racks. They might also be sent by their families on errands that required them to travel alone across the prairie to another camp as many as 30 miles away.

When they reached their late teens, Kit Foxes moved on to join the Stars.

With the counsel of this group's older adviser, the boys learned the Star Dance and the associated songs in preparation for the Star ceremony. The ceremony strengthened the bond among the group's members. As Starmen they would have more responsibilities in camp life. Membership in the Stars prepared them for entry into the four sacred lodges to which Arapaho men belonged.

A young Arapaho woman wearing a loose cloth dress, photographed by Edward S. Curtis in 1910. In their early teens, girls began to wear clothing that concealed their figures.

Old Crow (left), a tribal elder, announces that tribe member Little Raven, Jr. (right), is giving away a pony in honor of his child. This photograph was taken in 1901.

When a young man reached his twenties, he was allowed to go on his first buffalo hunt. He first invited several old men to a feast, where they instructed him and made his arrows, painting them with markings to identify their owner. The young hunter was told to give his first kill to an old man, who would pray for him. He might also be allowed by his elders to go into the hills to fast and pray, as part of what was called a vision quest—a search for a vision in which supernatural beings would promise special guidance. If he had such an experience, he was required to confide this to an old man

who supervised his spiritual development. During the course of several vision quests, a young man received instructions from the supernatural helper about either warfare or curing. The old man helped to interpret these instructions.

Before a man could marry, he had to show that he could support a wife and family. For this reason most men married when they were about 30 years old, by which time they might have achieved good military records, acquired horses by raiding other tribes, and in short gained the means to provide for their families. Young women, however, usually married in their late teens.

Although young women were discouraged from being near young men and were watched closely to prevent such contacts, they sometimes managed secret meetings. A young man might try to get the attention of a young woman by flashing a mirror or playing a flute outside her tipi. Or he might, while standing outside the tipi, take the poles that controlled the smoke flaps and move them so as to cause the tipi to fill with smoke. Then if the young woman's father or grandfather asked her to go outside to adjust the poles, the suitor would have a chance to talk with her briefly. A young man might also meet a young woman when she was sent to fetch water or go on another errand or when she visited one of his own female relatives.

Most marriages, however, were arranged by a young woman's older brother, father, or uncle. Her male relatives would choose a man they believed would be a good provider; often he was a friend of the brother. If a man admired a particular young woman, he might speak to her brother himself, or send his female relatives to ask her family for consent to the marriage. If a young woman disliked a man who was selected for her, she could refuse to marry him. This seldom happened, however, because her relatives invariably pressured her to agree to the family's wishes. No relatives could be considered as prospective husbands or

Ethnologist Truman Michelson, who lived among the Arapaho to study their ways in the early 1900s.

wives; the Arapaho considered their uncles and aunts to be as close in relationship as their own parents. In fact, the same term was used to describe a person's father and paternal uncle (father's brother). Similarly, a person's maternal aunts (mother's sisters) were referred to by the same term as the mother. There was no word for cousin—all the children of one's parents' brothers and sisters were considered the same as one's own brothers and sisters. Even people whose relationship was what we call second and third cousins were considered too closely related to marry.

An elderly Arapaho woman who was married in about 1868 told ethnologist Truman Michelson in 1932 how her marriage came about:

> Since I was not acquainted with the young man who became my husband, he sent his mother, two of his own sisters, and his paternal aunt to ask my brother and my maternal uncles for permission to marry me. My brother had given his consent before I was aware of it, as I happened to be away at the time. When I came to our tipi my brother came to me, which was unusual, sat near me and started to tell me what he had done, and that he had done so for the good of our father and mother. My father had expressed his willingness also. So when my mother started to talk to me, asking me to say what I thought, I told her that if my brother said it was all right, it would be all right with me, as I didn't want to hurt his feelings by refusing.

Another elderly woman, telling her girlhood experiences to anthropologist Inez Hilger in 1936, said that when her uncle arranged for her marriage against her wishes, she at first ran away:

> It was almost sundown. . . . I pulled my shawl over my head and face and cried, but kept on running. . . . It was getting dark. The owls were already hooting. I was "wild"! While I was still running, a horse passed me and circled around me. . . . A woman grabbed me, landed me on the horse, and took me back to camp. . . . I still insisted that I wasn't going to be married to him. . . . In the morning my uncles talked to me, and then I was willing to be married.

On the day of the wedding, the groom's family brought horses and other gifts to the bride's family, and the bride's family responded by giving an equivalent amount of property. After this exchange, the bride's family set up a tipi and furnished it, then invited the groom and his family there for a feast. At this feast the bride and groom sat together publicly for the first time, the marriage was announced, and elders prayed for the couple and instructed them on how to live a proper married life. The two families again exchanged presents, completing the marriage ceremony. Men gave horses and sometimes quivers (a case for carrying arrows), bows and arrows, and saddles. Women gave robes, clothing, and other household goods. Throughout the marriage, a woman retained her own property; she owned horses and the tipi and its furnishings.

Occasionally, when a family did not approve of a match, a couple would elope, much to the disapproval of the girl's family. When the couple returned and set up housekeeping, the husband might send a gift of horses to his wife's family so that the marriage was accepted, even if somewhat begrudgingly.

When a single man married, he hunted for game on behalf of his bride's family, and his mother-in-law cooked for the couple even if they had their own tipi. Only gradually did young women assume their full housekeeping responsibilities. If a man took a second wife, the senior or "boss" wife directed all the work of the household. Most men had two wives, and the most prosperous men had more, but before he took more than one, a man had to be able to provide for his wives and children. Usually a man who had more than one wife would marry a sister of his first wife, assuming that her family had found him to be a good husband. That way the wives would get along well with one another, and the husband's relationship with his in-laws was strengthened.

After marriage, the husband was expected to avoid his mother-in-law, and the wife her father-in-law. If they had to communicate, intermediaries were used. A teasing, joking relationship usually developed between a man and his wife's sisters and between a woman and her husband's brothers. Sometimes a husband's brother would rub soot on his fingers, steal into his sister-in-law's tipi, and blacken her nose and eyebrows while she slept. Brothers-in-law also teased each other. It was a favorite Arapaho joke for one to say the other was bowlegged because his mother had changed the dried manure in his cradle so rarely that it had become wadded like a ball between his knees. The butt of the joke might retort that his bowleggedness came from riding a horse as soon as he was able to walk.

There were four societies, or lodges, to which adult men could belong: the Tomahawk, Spear, Crazy, and Dog lodges. A man who was not initiated into the men's lodges could never be respected or obtain a position of responsibility. After completing the Star ceremony, young men seeking success in war or the restoration of health (whether their own or that of others) could vow to sponsor the next and more sacred ceremony of the Tomahawk Lodge. They were probably in their middle or late twenties when they did so. A vow to sponsor or the decision to participate in a lodge ceremony was considered a form of sacrificial prayer.

A young man who wanted to sponsor the Tomahawk Lodge ceremony would petition an older man (probably a Spearman in his thirties) to advise him and his fellow Starmen. Each candidate would seek out an older man, referred

A model of a Spear Lodge warrior. The crooked lance denotes special bravery and is wrapped with soft otter skin, which symbolizes protection from injury, and bound with sinew, which symbolizes strength.

to as a "Grandfather," who had completed the Tomahawk Lodge, and ask for instruction in the sacred songs and regalia. The Tomahawk Lodge ceremony, like that of the other three men's lodges, lasted for seven days and was held in the summer, when all the Arapaho were camped together. During the first three days, the young men were taught the secrets of the ceremony, and those who had been bravest in battle were chosen by the older men to carry special regalia in the coming dance. This honor recognized the courage of its recipients and at the same time obligated them to do even braver deeds. During the remaining four days, the men danced to the newly learned songs, which were actually prayers to the Creator. The ceremony was believed to confer great strength and potency on the young men. The Grandfather and his chosen grandson not only exchanged gifts but could thereafter never oppose each other. Either one could with propriety prevent the other from committing a violent act against another Arapaho; thus the relationship helped to keep peace in the camp.

As time passed, the young men of the Tomahawk Lodge gained experience in battle and took on increasing responsibilities in the camp. Eventually one would face danger or ill health and vow to sponsor the Spear Lodge—more sacred than the Tomahawk—in return for supernatural aid to get him out of his predicament. His fellow Tomahawkmen again joined him in seeking

Grandfathers, this time older men who had completed the Spear Lodge, to instruct them. As before, the first three days of the ceremony were spent in

A model of a Dog Lodge warrior. The stripes on the scarf draped over his chest symbolize the Four Hills of Life. The strands of buckskin on each side of the scarf represent the tribal elders known as the Seven Water-Pouring Old Men.

making regalia and learning songs. Again, the bravest men carried distinct regalia. In return, each honoree was expected one day to plant his lance in the earth during a battle and not retreat from it until it was removed by a fellow warrior. The Spear Lodge ceremony was considered to bestow overall success but especially supernatural aid in battle. In addition to serving as warriors, the Spearmen took on new responsibilities for keeping order in the camp and on the hunt and protecting their people when traveling across the open prairie. Most men married at about the time they entered the Spear Lodge.

Men who were about 40 years of age were considered mature enough to vow the Crazy Lodge. This lodge was more sacred than the Spear Lodge, and a man normally decided to vow it when he found himself sorely in need of supernatural aid. The vower and his fellow Spearmen would again choose Grandfathers who had already completed the Crazy ceremony. As before, the first three days of the ceremony were devoted to learning the songs and making the regalia of the dance that followed. The Crazymen carried small bows and arrows during the dance, and in the ceremony they were taught how to use the extract of a particular root on their arrows to paralyze animals and humans in the hunt or times of war. They also learned how to walk on hot coals and how to use a particular root to prevent fatigue. After pledging the Crazy Lodge, men had ceremonial duties; for

example, they assisted younger warriors' efforts to be successful in battle. The wives of candidates for the Crazy Lodge also participated in the ceremony of transfer, for the Crazy Lodge symbolically expressed the idea that life had male and female components, each necessary to the other.

When men reached their late forties or early fifties, it became appropriate to vow the Dog Lodge, the next and more sacred lodge in the series. Men who completed this ceremony directed battles and helped inspire younger warriors to brave deeds. Most leaders of the Arapaho bands were Dogmen. They and their wives acquired particularly great powers from their Grandfathers in this lodge—speed in battle, protection from bullets, and the ability to live into old age. At the age of about 60, Dogmen were eligible to join the Stoic Lodge of the old men.

Adult men of any age could pledge to sponsor or participate in the Offerings or Sacrifice Lodge, also known as the Sun Dance. This or one of the other men's lodges was held every summer. As required for the other lodges, a man needed a Grandfather for the Offerings Lodge. During the first three days of this ceremony the pledger was instructed in secret by elder ritual authorities. For the next four days the rest of the participants received instructions from their Grandfathers, fasted, and danced to exhaustion. The fasting and dancing were aspects of sacrifice. Another type of sacrifice was self-torture. A man tied one end of a thong to the

Participants in the Southern Arapaho Offerings or Sacrifice Lodge, photographed in Oklahoma in 1901 by George Dorsey. The Arapaho no longer allow this deeply revered ceremony to be photographed.

lodge's center pole, hooked the other end into his chest, and pulled away from the pole until his flesh tore. This was considered sacrificing a piece of flesh. The Sacrifice Lodge was the most respected of the prayer-sacrifice rites because it called for both immense physical suffering and large donations of property on the part of the dancers and their families. The Sacrifice Lodge symbolically expressed events in Arapaho mythology. It was believed to assist the physical and spiritual well-being of all Arapaho, and its successful

completion required harmony and co-operation. Each time a man participated in a ceremony he gained ritual knowledge, prestige, and authority. He could serve as Grandfather to a younger man or direct some phase of that ceremony.

A man might also obtain supernatural power for his personal use by petitioning the Creator for contact with a supernatural being. The degree and kind of power characteristic of each type of supernatural being varied, but the Creator's agents could confer the ability to cure sickness, to assure success in war and other ventures, to control the weather, and to foretell the future. A man seeking supernatural power fasted alone on a hill or mountain peak, concentrating his thoughts and making offerings over a period of one to seven days. If he were successful, a supernatural being came to him, usually in the form of an animal that changed into human form and gave him specific powers. The seeker also received instructions in how to use his power, a song associated with the power, and an object or objects that symbolized or served as a vehicle of the power. Some men had dreams in which supernatural beings appeared, without having been sought, and offered them power. Sometimes a man refused power, for it had the potential to harm the recipient or his relatives if misused. Power was supposed to be used only for good; sorcery, the use of supernatural power for evil purposes, could cause harm to its owner as well as to intended victims. A man carried his

A model of the shield of Sitting Eagle, made before 1900. Shields were decorated with objects or designs seen in a vision quest. A supernatural helper appeared to Sitting Eagle in the form of a bear, symbolizing ferocity in battle. The shield has been ornamented with two bear claws from which eagle feathers hang.

power objects in a medicine bag and sometimes painted images from his vision on his tipi, or, if his power was for war, on his shield. He might also wear power objects, such as feathers. A man could give or sell his supernatural power to another person, along with the instructions for its use and the medicine bag objects that related to it.

In warfare men sought to do brave deeds. This might involve killing an enemy in a way that brought personal risk. Rushing into the fray and striking an enemy, stealing horses from inside an enemy camp, and taking a scalp or other war trophy from an enemy also involved risk, and these deeds were as esteemed as killing an enemy, if not more so. Performing any of these activities entitled a man to take a new name commemorating his deed and to paint his exploits on his tipi lining or his shirt.

Men wore their hair in a way that symbolized their bravery in war. Early in the century, they wore their hair parted on each side and standing upright in the center over the forehead. Over their temples it was cut into a zigzag edge. In front of their ears the hair hung down, either braided or tied together. They thought that wearing the hair upright over the forehead made them look fierce. Later, men braided the hair or tied it in masses over their ears and kept a scalp lock in the center at the back of their head. They tied feathers or other objects symbolic of their supernatural helpers onto the hair.

Performing brave deeds helped a man build a reputation and gain prestige. For example, acquiring a large number of horses through raiding enabled a man not only to support a large household but to be generous to others, and public generosity was requisite to leadership. If a man donated to ceremonies and gave generously to elders, widows, and orphans and if he was even-tempered and competent, he might be selected by other men and elders to become the leader of his band.

Decisions for the camp as a whole were generally made by consensus among the adult men and some of the elderly women. Elderly ritual authorities and the leaders of the men's lodges were particularly influential. It was the ential men could rely on the men of the lodges to enforce decisions if necessary. A lodge could, for example, destroy a man's personal belongings and even kill his horse for violating the rules of a hunt.

Elder women, like elder men, had authority in religious matters, and older women had considerable influence over family affairs. At every age, a woman could help her husband improve his position and at the same time gain prestige for herself and her children in a number of ways. She could make prayer-sacrifices of property; wives often gave away their own property generously to others on behalf of their husbands (and sometimes brothers). She could vow to sponsor or participate in the women's sacred Buffalo Lodge, which was believed to help ensure success in the buffalo hunt. She could also offer physical suffering on behalf of family members.

One woman told Truman Michelson of the circumstances behind her own sacrifice. When her sister became ill and two of the best Arapaho doctors failed to cure her, she explained:

A model of White Buffalo Woman, a leader of the women's Buffalo Lodge, which held ceremonies to ensure success in the hunt. Her face is painted white and she holds a whistle in her mouth to lure the buffalo, which provided food, hides and other raw materials that the Arapaho used to make many essential articles.

> I unhesitatingly made a vow to sacrifice my left little finger, so that my sister's life might be spared, so that her small children, who were a pitiful sight to me as they were about their helpless mother, might again enjoy happiness. . . . The next morning an Arapaho woman was called to remove my finger in the usual way. . . . My sister commenced to get better, improving very quickly.

band leader's job to gain a consensus and then to persuade others to abide by that consensus. He and the other influ-

Women made designs using quills and beads that served as prayers for the well-being of their owner on garments and other household objects. When they made moccasins, for example, they would often work prayers in symbolic form into the design.

Women could also acquire through dreams the individually owned supernatural power to use herbs for healing; in the dreams they were shown what plants to use and how to use them. A man could also give his individually owned supernatural power to his wife. Women made essential contributions to all of the tribal ceremonies by preparing the food considered essential to the establishment and maintenance of relationships between Grandfather and Grandson, priest and devotee, and humans and the Creator.

Maintaining the Arapaho's good standing with the Creator was primarily the responsibility of old people, particularly the elderly ritual authorities. Most prominent among these were the Stoic Lodge members, the seven Water-Pouring Old Men, and the keeper of the Flat Pipe bundle.

Men of 60 or so completed the Stoic Lodge. This ceremony involved four nights of fasting and prayer led by seven tribal priests called Water-Pouring Old Men and was so sacred that young people did not go near it. The Stoicmen had the responsibility of praying for the well-being of all Arapaho and were supposed to think only good thoughts. "Whatever they prayed for was thought to be granted," one Arapaho told anthropologist Inez Hilger.

The Stoicmen had the right and duty to paint the people with sacred red paint, which in a variety of ways "renewed the happiness of thought and mind in the people," as one said to Hilger. They painted the faces of mourners, for example, to reintegrate them into the society after the period of mourning was over. Just as the newborn baby was painted with the red sacred paint, the body, face, and hair of a dead person were painted before burial. Elders applied red paint to their own faces daily. The paint symbolized old age, sacredness, and earth or subsistence; thus the very appearance of the aged reminded other Arapaho of the elders' central role in the tribe's well-being.

The seven Water-Pouring Old Men also directed all the lodge ceremonies. These elderly ritual leaders wore their hair uncombed and gathered in a bunch over the forehead. Every day when the tribe was camped together, they prayed in a large domed lodge, called a sweat lodge, in the center of the camp circle. Inside the sweat lodge, they poured water over hot coals to make steam, which helped their prayers ascend to the Creator. Each Water-Pouring Old Man was custodian of a bag containing a rattle and sacred paint. The rattle was used in prayer-songs and the paint in all religious ceremonies. Symbolically, these seven men represented the former custodians of the Flat Pipe bundle,

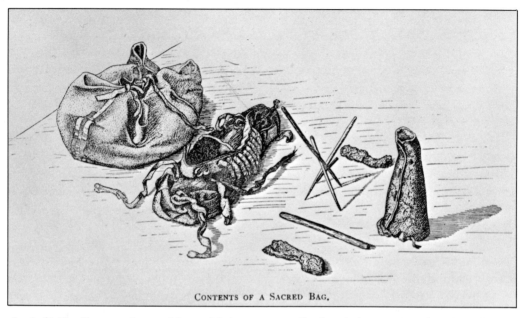

CONTENTS OF A SACRED BAG.

An individually-owned sacred bag with its contents displayed, in an 1899 drawing. From left to right are the outer bag, holding gifts of food; an inner bag; two small bags of incense, called "man" and "woman"; a stick, representing the gift of a horse; an arrangement of four small sticks, representing a tipi; and a standing leather cone, the spirit of the bag itself. Gifts of food and cloth offered to the bag were believed to insure prosperity for the giver.

central to the Arapaho creation myth, and they were responsible for helping to conduct ceremonies involving the Flat Pipe.

The Flat Pipe bundle itself was in the custody of an old man known as the keeper. He represented the First Pipe Keeper, the mythological being who had been given the Pipe on behalf of the Arapaho, and was himself regarded as sacred. The keeper conducted rites to ensure the annual renewal of the earth and the continued prosperity of the tribe. He used his authority to generate consensus and resolve conflict.

The Flat Pipe bundle was referred to as "Old Man" and kept in a special tipi, painted with sacred designs, that stood in the center of the camp circle. In addition to the Pipe, the bundle contained other objects that represented events in the creation story. It was suspended on a stand of four sticks. Proper care of the Pipe was necessary to maintain a harmonious relationship with the Creator and nature. If the Pipe were destroyed, an earthquake or flood would follow. Arapaho who wished to make prayers to the Creator through the Flat Pipe could accompany their prayers with a sacrifice of property, usually robes.

Later the keeper distributed these offerings to the needy.

Like the seven tribal bags kept by the Water-Pouring Old Men, there were seven sacred bags kept by seven old women. These bags held incense and implements for painting and quill embroidery. The seven women attained their positions by fasting and other kinds of sacrifice. Using the sacred objects in their bags, they supervised the embroidery of tipi ornaments and the decoration of buffalo robes and cradles. They prayed that the designs, which represented prayers for health and long life, would be executed correctly and accomplish the desired ends. Men were excluded from these rites.

Old people, both male and female, had extensive authority not only in ceremonies but in the daily lives of children, youths, and mature adults. They gave frequent orations praising noteworthy individuals and supporting the actions of tribal leaders. Younger Arapaho usually followed their elders' wishes, and relied constantly on their knowledge and prayers, believing that elders were most qualified to mediate between the people and the Creator.

In the mid-19th century, however, the spiritual beliefs of the Arapaho, as well as their way of life, would come under assault as intruders entered their territory and altered forever the world as the Arapaho knew it. ▲

A Northern Arapaho family preparing a meal. Metal containers obtained from non-Indian traders replaced pottery and other Indian-made utensils in the late 19th century.

THE STRUGGLE
TO SURVIVE

Before 1841 the Arapaho depended on hunting buffalo to provide the basis of their subsistence. By hunting small game and collecting edible plant foods they rounded out their diet. From plant and animal materials available in their environment they made almost everything else they needed. Since the early 19th century they had been in contact with traders, to whom they gave buffalo robes in exchange for manufactured goods, which were luxuries for them. Arapaho women prized red, white, and blue glass beads, woolen trade cloth, metal cooking pots, brass wire for bracelets, and Navajo blankets. Arapaho men sought metal knives, tobacco, iron for arrowheads, and, above all, guns and ammunition to defend themselves against enemy tribes to the east that already possessed firearms.

In the 1840s, emigrants from the eastern United States began traveling westward through Arapaho country on their way to what are now the states of Oregon, California, and Utah. At first they followed the Oregon Trail along the North Platte River, through what is now Wyoming, to Sweetwater River and into Utah. In 1848, the United States successfully concluded a two-year war against Mexico to expand its southwestern frontier. As a result, emigrant travel on the Santa Fe Trail increased dramatically after 1848, as travelers streamed westward through what is now Kansas, across the Arkansas River, and southwest to Santa Fe. After the discovery of gold in California in 1849, there was a significant increase in traffic along the Platte River route.

An early result of these intrusions was the disruption of the migratory pattern of the buffalo herds on which the Arapaho depended. Ultimately, the buffalo population declined drastically. Before the 19th century was over, American westward expansion would threaten the Arapaho's very survival.

Explorer John C. Frémont noted that in the 1820s and 1830s large herds of buffalo were never out of a traveler's view from the Rocky Mountains to the Missouri River. Gradually the herds came to occupy more restricted territory, moving into areas away from the lanes of travel. Medicine Man, a representative of the Northern Arapaho in the late 1850s and 1860s, spoke to federal officials about the tribe's plight:

Salt meadows on the Upper Missouri, and great herds of buffalo, *drawn by George Catlin around 1832. The artist wrote, "We stood amazed at the almost incredible numbers [of buffalo], large masses of black, most pleasingly to contrast with the snow white and the vivid green." Half a century later the great herds had been hunted to near extinction, threatening the survival of the Plains Indians as well.*

Our country for hunting game has become very small. We see the white men everywhere. Their rifles kill some of the game, and the smoke of their campfires scares the rest away. . . . It is but a few years ago when we encamped here, in this valley of Deer Creek, and remained many moons, for the buffalo were plenty, and made the prairie look black all around us. Now none are to be seen. . . . Our old people and little children are hungry for many days . . . for our hunters can get no meat. Our sufferings are increasing every winter. Our horses are dying because we ride them so far to get a little game for our lodges. We wish to live.

Despite these provocations, the Arapaho did not attack the wagon trains. As the buffalo became scarce, however, competition escalated among Indian tribes over hunting territory. To defend themselves the Arapaho, along with their allies, the Cheyenne, needed guns and ammunition that could be obtained only through trade. They especially desired new rifles such as those possessed by Indians who lived farther east. They quickly recognized that it was not in their best interest to drive away traders and others who had the goods they wanted. Instead, the Arapaho found it more practical to refrain from attacks and extract "presents" from travelers in return for letting them pass through without being molested. Wagon trains along the Arkansas and Platte river routes were confronted with long lines of mounted warriors waving American flags and bearing letters from officials attesting to their good character. The Indians solicited arms, ammunition, and luxuries such as tobacco, sugar, bread, and coffee in return for the safe passage of the wagon trains.

The people on these wagon trains often carried published guidebooks that advised them how to have a safe trip. One, entitled the *Parsons Guidebook*, stressed that when travelers reached Arapaho and Cheyenne country, they would encounter Indians desiring supplies. Treat them well, advised the guidebook: if three or four, feed them; if in bands of two or three hundred, feed the chief men.

Several Arapaho leaders developed reputations among the travelers as "friendly chiefs." They would approach the caravans dressed in military uniforms, wearing medals given them by government officials and carrying documents that introduced them as "friendly." These credentials entitled them to receive gifts and hospitality from the travelers. The friendly chiefs used their privileged status to attract and hold on to the loyalty of their followers. They distributed the gifts they received to their followers. This was in full accord with Arapaho tradition: To be accepted as a leader, to gain prestige,

South Pass Gateway of the Rockies, an 1837 painting by William Henry Jackson. This region, in what is now Wyoming, was within the homeland of the Northern Arapaho.

one had to be generous to others. Some of the friendly chiefs, such as Friday of the Northern Arapaho and Left Hand of the Southern Arapaho, became fluent in English, which helped them represent their people to the American travelers and government officials.

Friday had been named Black Spot at birth. While still a child, he was inadvertently left behind one day in 1831 when his people moved camp. He wandered for days until the trapper and trader Thomas Fitzpatrick found him on the Cimarron River in southeastern Colorado. Fitzpatrick named the boy Friday, for the day on which he found him. The trader became so fond of young Friday that he took him to St. Louis to live with him. He also sent Friday to school for two years, where he learned English. Until 1838 Friday stayed with the trader, traveling west into Indian country with him and becoming accustomed to and learning about the Americans, or "mysterious ones," as the Arapaho called them. On one of these trips west in 1838, they entered a camp of Northern Arapaho, and Friday, now a young man, was recognized by his relatives. He then rejoined his people, taking his place as a hunter and warrior. One of Fitzpatrick's contemporaries wrote: "Few Indians or whites can compete with Friday as a buffalo-hunter, either in the use of the bow or rifle. I have seen him kill five of these animals at a single chase, and am informed that he has not infrequently exceeded that number."

As a young warrior, Friday began to build a reputation for bravery against the Arapaho's enemies, the Pawnee, Shoshone, and Ute. In one fight with the Ute he engaged a warrior in hand-to-hand combat, snatched the warrior's loaded gun away when it failed to fire, and then killed him. He and others in the war party destroyed a village of seven tipis that day. Fighting against the Pawnee, he shot a pony out from under a man in the thickest part of the fight.

But Friday's renown among his people came primarily from his skill as an interpreter and intermediary. Comfortable with the Americans, he smoothed over quarrels and misunderstandings, and on more than one occasion prevented attacks on the Arapaho. Friday interpreted for John Frémont and other explorers, and for army officers sent to keep peace along the emigration routes in the 1840s. He also served as interpreter to Little Owl, the Northern Arapaho chief in the 1850s, and to his successor, Medicine Man.

Less is known of Left Hand. He apparently made a trip east of the Missouri in the 1850s, when he was middle-aged, and seems to have received instruction in English before then. In 1859 he was recognized by settlers and government officials as an important Southern Arapaho leader who visited them frequently and tried to maintain good relations between his people and theirs.

Friday, a renowned "friendly chief" of the Northern Arapaho. This daguerreotype was probably taken while he was with a delegation to Washington, D.C., in 1851–52, after the signing of the Treaty of Fort Laramie.

The U.S. government was eager to encourage settlement of the West. Officials were concerned about the hazards posed to emigrants by clashes among various warring tribes and between the Indians and the emigrants

themselves. In 1846, Thomas Fitzpatrick was appointed federal Indian agent for the Arapaho and other tribes along and between the Platte and Arkansas rivers. Fitzpatrick, who was well respected by the Arapaho, sought their continued goodwill by visiting them and distributing gifts of sugar and coffee. He urged them not to retaliate against the travelers who were damaging their buffalo range. Shortly after becoming agent, Fitzpatrick married Margaret Poisal, the daughter of an American trader and Left Hand's sister. Fitzpatrick's marriage to Left Hand's niece further cemented his relationship with the tribe.

A few years later, his superiors in Washington, D.C., instructed him to arrange a council between representatives of the federal government and of the tribes under his jurisdiction. They hoped to obtain an agreement that the tribes would remain in well-defined areas of occupation in order to minimize conflicts that threatened the safe passage of homesteaders.

The site selected for the treaty council was on Horse Creek, 35 miles east of Fort Laramie. On August 31, 1851, the Indians began arriving—10,000 Arapaho, Cheyenne, Sioux, and a few Crow, Shoshone, and others from north of the Platte. In all, most of the Plains Indians were represented. The horse herds were so large that in only a few days the grass was stripped away for miles around by their grazing. To the amazement of the officials, no fights broke out, even between tribes that routinely battled one another. All had made a sacred pledge to keep the peace. Each tribe put on displays of horsemanship and battle skills. Feasts were held during the day, and dances at night, while the Indian leaders talked to the officials from Washington.

On September 17, the Indians signed a treaty in which they agreed to curtail war parties, refrain from attacking U.S. citizens, and allow military posts to be built in Indian territory. Each tribe was assigned a particular tract of land as its primary residence,

although hunting and traveling outside these tracts was permitted. The Arapaho, along with the Cheyenne, were acknowledged to have control over the area between the North Platte and Arkansas rivers west to the foothills of the Rocky Mountains. During the council, each tribe chose intermediary chiefs, leaders whom the U.S. could consider representatives. The Arapaho selected Little Owl, a well-known friendly chief of the Northern Arapaho, to be their primary spokesman; they also selected the Southern Arapaho chiefs Cut Nose and Big Man. The Arapaho expected

"Friendly" chiefs photographed near the Rocky Mountains around 1859. Friday is on the right; the man next to him is probably Little Owl. The other two are unidentified. All wear traditional buffalo robes.

these leaders to express the wishes of the group as a whole, not to make agreements on their own. In return for their concessions, all of the Indians at the Horse Creek council were promised an annual distribution of blankets, cloth, clothing, metal utensils and tools, and guns and ammunition.

After these intermediary chiefs signed the treaty, presents were distributed. The most important men each received a major general's uniform and a medal; other influential men received similar, though less impressive, gifts. One of the soldiers at the treaty council described a newly bedecked chief:

Wearing a saber, [and a] medal with the head of the President on one side and clasped hands on the other, he carries a document with an immense seal and ribbon thereon—enclosed in a large envelope, that he may show all comers what the Great Father [the President] thinks of him—what rank and power he wields among his fellow man.

Twenty-seven wagonloads of presents—including tobacco, cloth, paint, blankets, knives, beads, sugar, and coffee—were delivered to the designated chiefs, and each distributed the presents among the people of his tribe. Delegates, Friday among them, were also chosen to go east to meet with President Millard Fillmore. They returned from Washington with gifts from the president, including a flag and a medal for each. They also came back with the clear realization that if the Arapaho of-

fered military opposition to western expansion, they would be destroyed by a larger and more technologically advanced society.

There was another reason why the Arapaho needed to remain on good terms with the Americans. As wild game became more and more scarce, the Indians came to rely increasingly on gifts of manufactured goods. At first such gifts were regarded as luxuries, but by the 1860s they had become necessities. Hunters could no longer find enough buffalo to make tribal clothing and robes to trade for goods. The Arapaho came to depend on the Indian agent, who distributed large quantities of blankets, different kinds of cloth, needles, thread, shirts, shawls, ribbon, beads, vermilion (a red pigment used as paint or dye), and brass wire, as well as a few hats, umbrellas, and handkerchiefs that were sought for their prestige value. Good conduct also brought from the agent a large annual reward of percussion and flintlock rifles. Although the bow and arrow was very efficient for hunting buffalo, these guns were essential for hunting the smaller game upon which the tribe increasingly relied.

The Arapaho's situation became particularly precarious in the 1850s because the heartland of their hunting territory—the western portion of the land designated in 1851 for the Cheyenne and the Arapaho—became flooded with emigrant caravans and settlers. In 1856, Americans began to settle permanently in the Smoky Hill River valley, one of the few remaining buffalo ranges. In 1858, prospectors joining the gold rush to the Pike's Peak area in Colorado took over the Arapaho's favorite campsites along the headwaters of the South Platte and in the Parks.

Denver and other towns quickly appeared. Despite the 1851 treaty, which permitted homesteaders only passage through the Indians' land, not permanent occupancy, the federal government made no effort to halt the growth of the towns. The government counted on the gold from these areas to develop the nation's economy.

The spread of the towns brought about a crucial event in Arapaho history: the splitting of the tribe into two divisions, northern and southern. Before settlements became extensive, bands of Arapaho in the north had roamed what is now Colorado and southern Wyoming, whereas those in the south had ranged between the South Platte and Arkansas rivers. The incursions of miners and homesteaders drove the northern-ranging bands still farther north, whereas those in the south tried to stay below the increasingly crowded Denver area. By 1855,

Denver, drawn here as it appeared around 1858, was a frontier town of travelers, wagons, settlers, cabins, gold seekers, tents, and Southern Arapaho lodges.

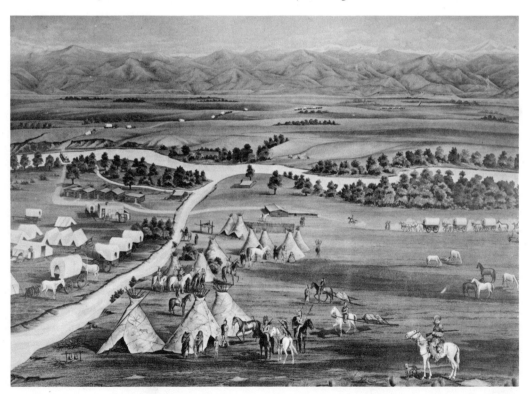

THE DIVISION OF THE ARAPAHO

the two divisions were politically self-contained and independent of each other, and each had its own Indian agent assigned by the federal government. Separation was a gradual process, but it ultimately brought about differing identities for the two divisions. The Northern Arapaho formed an alliance with the Sioux and Northern Cheyenne and were able to hunt in what is now Wyoming and Montana, an area that was sparsely populated and hence less threatening to their existence. The Southern Arapaho, dwelling in what became Colorado and Kansas, had more interest in accommodating the new settlers. By the early 1860s, these settlers outnumbered the Southern Arapaho 10 to 1. The potential for conflict between the settlers and the Arapaho was great. The settlers' livestock was a temptation to the tribe, which was often short of food, particularly after diseases brought by the immigrants killed many hunters. When the Sioux and Cheyenne were goaded into skirmishes with government troops in 1854 and 1856, respectively, all Indians, including the Arapaho, were in danger of being fired upon by troops and civilians alike. The Arapaho were remarkably successful in avoiding the hostilities, however. They restricted their movements to areas away from trouble spots, and the lodges helped older leaders control the young warriors, who were eager to retaliate for the intruders' depredations.

Actually, the Arapaho were attracted to the settlements for practical reasons, and instigating hostilities would have been against their best interests. They came to trade for sugar and coffee, and the miners and settlers often gave them gifts and food. When Arapaho men went to war against the Ute, they left their families camped near the settlements for safety. Little Raven, the Southern Arapaho intermediary chief in 1860, his interpreter Left Hand, and other distinguished warriors and leaders were invited to dinner parties

by the business leaders and officials of the new towns.

But the Arapaho leaders realized that they could not survive if the settlements continued to expand and threaten their hunting way of life. In 1860 Friday was heard to say plaintively, "The Great Spirit must have turned himself white and given white people power equal to his own." The intermediary chiefs asked for a new treaty, one that would guarantee them

Little Raven, a Southern Arapaho intermediary chief, photographed in New York in 1871.

a place in their own country where they would not be encroached upon by their white neighbors.

The Northern Arapaho, who reportedly numbered about 750 in 1861, wanted to stay on the lands they had found north of the Southern division. The Southern Arapaho, who numbered approximately 1,500, were now located primarily south of Denver. Both divisions had suffered severe population losses due to epidemics of smallpox and cholera and a shortage of food.

On February 18, 1861, Southern Arapaho Indian agent Albert Boone, a grandson of the famed frontier adventurer and settler Daniel Boone, held a council that was attended by some bands of Southern Arapaho and a few Cheyenne. He later reported that he had obtained their consent to the cession of most of their territory, reserving for them a small reservation on Colorado's Sand Creek, away from areas of white settlement. The Cheyenne were to occupy the eastern half, and both divisions of the Arapaho the western. However, it is unclear whether the Arapaho understood the conditions of this treaty. Their chief interpreter, Left Hand, was not present. Moreover, the Sand Creek reservation provided no way for them to hunt, because the buffalo range was east and north of the reservation, and it seems unlikely they would have knowingly accepted this limitation. In any case, the Northern division did not consent to the cession. By 1862 the Southern Arapaho were in such dire circumstances—due largely to the loss of buffalo at the hands of professional hunters—that, although there were no attacks on settlers, Little Raven and other leaders could no longer keep their people from stealing the settlers' livestock.

Still the Southern Arapaho worked to convince the Cheyenne to join them in remaining at peace with the whites. But, as hard as they tried, eventually they were unable to avoid conflict. In the spring of 1864, in retaliation for suspected rustling, Colorado troops destroyed a Cheyenne village, killing women and children, and, in another instance, shot two friendly chiefs. The Cheyenne replied in kind by attacking Colorado settlements. Officials there determined to forcibly drive all Indians away from areas of settlement and travel routes or, failing that, to exterminate them. The army began to relentlessly attack Cheyenne villages, even those that had remained at peace.

These attacks brought retaliation from the Cheyenne and eventually involved the Arapaho. Initially, Little Raven, with Left Hand's help, tried desperately to avoid hostilities. They preferred to have the tribe depend increasingly on rations provided by the army rather than risk hunting in settlement areas, where they were in danger of being attacked. Only small war parties of Arapaho made occasional raids.

John Evans, governor of the area (known as the Colorado Territory), ordered all friendly Indians to designated areas near army posts, where he guaranteed them safety, and ordered that

Indians outside the designated areas be hunted down. Despite the governor's commands, army officers frequently ordered Indians away from the posts. When Left Hand, carrying a white flag, approached Fort Larned to offer to help retrieve lost army livestock, he was fired on.

In September a large number of Arapaho, and some Cheyenne under Black Kettle, were ordered to camp near Fort Lyon on Sand Creek, where they were guaranteed protection. All had pledged peace and delivered up captives, arms, and booty. There were 500 Indians—about 110 tipis of Cheyenne, led by Black Kettle, and 8 tipis of Arapaho, led by Left Hand—already there. On November 29, 1864, Colonel John Chivington led a group of the Colorado militia in a surprise attack on the Indian encampment. At least 130 people, mostly women and children, were killed. Left Hand was among them.

The main body of the Southern Arapaho, led by Little Raven, were in a large camp several miles from Sand Creek. This group—composed mostly of women, children, and the elderly— escaped south and took refuge in Kiowa and Comanche country. Most Arapaho men, upon hearing of the massacre, joined the Cheyenne in an all-out war against whites that lasted through the spring of 1865. Despite the Arapaho's peaceful disposition, the massacre, said Little Raven, "was too bad to stand."

In the summer of 1865, Arapaho leaders, with Little Raven as spokesman, began trying to arrange a truce and obtain a reservation where they could live undisturbed by whites. A council of federal officials, Southern Cheyenne, and Southern Arapaho was held October 11, with Thomas Fitzpatrick's widow, Margaret, interpreting for the Arapaho at their request. The Southern Arapaho disassociated themselves from both their Northern tribesmen and the Cheyenne, believing this would help them gain a reservation, and reiterated their desire for peace. Yet when the Cheyenne and the army attacked each other during the winter of 1866–67, all Arapaho were at risk, for the army did not always distinguish between friendly and hostile Indians; moreover, most whites in the area considered the Arapaho as guilty as the Cheyenne for raids on settlements and wagon trains. Many Arapaho bands remained south of the Arkansas River, away from the fighting.

Observers at the Sand Creek massacre had reported to newspapers in eastern cities that the militia had savagely mutilated men, women, and children, shot unarmed people in the process of surrendering, and committed other atrocities. In response to the public outcry, in order to avoid a costly and prolonged war with the Indians, President Andrew Johnson authorized a peace commission, despite the army's objections. A treaty council was held at Medicine Lodge Creek in the fall of 1867.

Although some Cheyenne tried to discourage them, the Southern Arapaho attended the council and insisted

An artist from Frank Leslie's Illustrated Newspaper *drew this scene of Southern Arapaho and Comanche at the treaty council at Medicine Lodge Creek, on October 19, 1867.*

on being dealt with separately from their neighbors. Little Raven and others wanted land in Colorado but eventually agreed to accept instead a reservation in Kansas, between the Arkansas and the Cimarron rivers, which they would receive when claims to the area were relinquished by other tribes. The Arapaho were dissatisfied with this area, however, and over the next two years they tried to persuade officials to grant them a reservation on the North Canadian River. They knew they would not be safe on the Arkansas River while the Cheyenne and the U. S. troops continued to fight there and the army per-

sisted in attacking peaceful Indians. In the meantime, most of the Southern Arapaho fled to the Wichita Mountains to avoid contact with the army.

In the winter of 1869, Little Raven came to Fort Sill (located in what is now Oklahoma) and, insisting that his people had always kept the peace, "surrendered" to the army, thus placing the Southern Arapaho under government protection. Officials at Fort Sill, convinced that the Arapaho's leaders could control the young warriors, sent Little Raven's group to the Camp Supply area, where it was still possible to hunt. President Ulysses Grant sent Quaker

Indian agent Brinton Darlington to protect their interests and by executive order granted the Arapaho and Cheyenne a reservation together, in Oklahoma Territory on the Canadian River. Still hoping to disassociate themselves from the Cheyenne, the Southern Arapaho (who now numbered 1,100 to 1,500) began to move to the vicinity of this new reservation and receive regular rations of sugar, coffee, and other goods.

By this time, most of the Northern Arapaho had withdrawn north of the Platte River, avoiding trouble and hunting the remaining buffalo in what is now Wyoming and Montana. They had also formed an alliance with Sioux and Northern Cheyenne in an attempt to protect their hunting territory from incursions by whites and by other tribes.

But gold was discovered in Montana in 1862, and military posts and settlements inevitably followed. The result,

aggravated by the Sand Creek massacre, was a war that lasted from 1865 to 1868, at which time President Grant's peace commission met with the Northern Arapaho and their allies. Battered by their losses, the Northern Arapaho agreed to settle on a reservation with either the Sioux in the north or the Southern Arapaho in Oklahoma. The government agreed to close their military posts and to bar settlers and travelers from the tribes' hunting territory. The Northern Arapaho, however, were determined to obtain their own reservation in Wyoming, separate from that of the Sioux, and their leaders began to develop relations with army officers at Fort Fetterman in order to achieve that goal.

The two most important Northern Arapaho leaders were Medicine Man and Black Bear. They sent for Friday, an accomplished interpreter and es-

Southern Arapaho and Cheyenne await the distribution of rations at their new home at Camp Supply, Oklahoma Territory, in 1870. The Indians surround the field where flour, sugar, bacon, coffee, and tobacco were piled for distribution by band chiefs under the supervision of Indian agent Brinton Darlington and military officers.

teemed tribal member, to help them develop good relations with the army. After 1868, the Northern Arapaho began serving regularly as scouts to the army and returning lost livestock to the troops. They also sought to establish peaceful relations with their longtime enemies, the Shoshone (who had accepted a reservation in Wyoming in 1868), and army officers made appropriate arrangements to help them to that end. For a short time the Northern Arapaho lived on the Shoshone reservation, but there were clashes with trespassing settlers and miners along the Sweetwater and Popoagie rivers.

After Black Bear was ambushed and killed by a mob of settlers, Medicine Man led the tribe back to the vicinity of Fort Fetterman and resumed efforts to obtain a reservation solely for the Northern Arapaho. Game was so scarce that they depended on the army's issues of canvas to make their tipis, cloth for their clothing, and rations for their sustenance. Medicine Man died in 1871

Northern Arapaho and their allies meet with U.S. Peace Commission officials at Fort Laramie, Wyoming, in May 1868. The Arapaho agreed to move to a reservation, and the government agreed to keep settlers out of the Indians' hunting territory.

Black Coal, principal chief of the Northern Arapaho following the death of Medicine Man, photographed in 1882.

and was succeeded by Black Coal. In 1874 a combined force of troops and Shoshone warriors—the Arapaho's traditional enemies—attacked a large Northern Arapaho camp in Central Wyoming. Most of their tipis, horses, and winter provisions were destroyed or stolen. Now the Northern Arapaho were totally dependent on the inadequate rations they obtained at Red Cloud, the Sioux Agency. Every 10 days they received 4 days' rations. Many people died of illness and exposure in 1875 and 1876.

In the fall of 1876 the government called the Northern Arapaho, Northern Cheyenne, and Sioux together at the Sioux's Red Cloud Agency in Nebraska to negotiate the cession of the Black Hills in Wyoming and South Dakota. The tribes had little choice but to sign on the government's terms. Winter was coming; if they refused they would receive no provisions. Nonetheless, Black Coal told the officials from Washington that the Northern Arapaho were unwilling to settle in Oklahoma, as the government had proposed. After he made a trip to inspect the Southern Arapaho reservation on the Canadian River, Black Coal was more determined than ever to find a way for his people to remain in Wyoming.

Black Coal and other Arapaho leaders found a strategy that eventually proved successful: Virtually all their warriors signed on as army scouts in 1876 and 1877, assisting the army in defeating Northern Cheyenne and Sioux bands that continued to refuse to settle on a reservation. Serving as "scout chiefs" enabled men to build reputations for generosity and bravery, to earn prestige and authority. The Northern Arapaho scouts wore army uniforms as well as feathered headdresses that testified to feats of courage and symbolized personal "war medicine" obtained in a vision quest. They received soldiers' pay, material provisions, rations, guns, and ammunition and could keep property seized from the enemy. This provided them with enough food and goods to enable them to be generous to others. The strategy devised by Black Coal and other Arapaho leaders proved effective: The scout chiefs gained the respect of army officers and obtained their promise to help the tribe settle in Wyoming. Sharp Nose rose to prominence as a leader of scouts, and he and Black Coal became the leading intermediary chiefs. To the Northern Arapaho, the scout uniform symbolized their bravery and generosity; to whites, it represented the Indians' trustworthiness and loyalty to the federal government.

In 1877, the Northern Arapaho were permitted to send a delegation to meet with President Rutherford Hayes in Washington, D.C. Black Coal, Sharp Nose, and Friday went, accompanied by army officers. Black Coal told President Hayes:

> Last summer I went to see [the Southern Arapaho-Southern Cheyenne reservation]. . . . Southern Arapahos, they told me it was sickly in that country. . . . They said a good many had died since that they had been there. . . . When I came home I told my people what I heard; and they said . . . "Now you must push and talk for us, for we want to stay in this country [Wyoming]."

With the army's help, the three Northern Arapaho delegates obtained permission for their people to settle on the Shoshone reservation in Wyoming. The delegates returned in triumph, wearing suits and medals given them by President Hayes, and riding in a black wagon filled with presents. To the Arapaho, the black paint symbolized a victory in an encounter with an enemy. In March 1878 Black Coal and Sharp Nose arrived on the Shoshone reservation with their people. ▲

An Arapaho man and his child, with equipment used during the peyote ritual, including a rattle and a feathered fan. The young girl wears a blouse decorated with elk's teeth.

MAKING ADJUSTMENTS: THE NORTHERN ARAPAHO,

1878–1964

When the Northern Arapaho arrived at the Wind River reservation in Wyoming in the spring of 1878, they faced new challenges. The first was how to survive when there was little game and the government provided only inadequate rations. The second was how to safeguard their new home when they had no treaty rights there and the legal owners, the Shoshone, did not want them as permanent residents. The last was how to survive as Arapaho, meeting their traditional obligations to kin and to supernatural forces, when the government's policy was to replace their culture with that of the mainstream non-Indian society.

These three problems were interrelated, for the government threatened to withhold food and remove the tribe from the reservation if they tried to maintain their Arapaho traditions. The Arapaho, however, felt that abandonment of their religious responsibilities would jeopardize both their survival and their political status on the reservation. To cope with any one of these problems, they had to cope with all three.

After defeating the Plains tribes militarily and confining them to reservations, the government had embarked on a program to "civilize" the Plains tribes by teaching them to farm, speak English, and accept Christianity. Yet Congress did not provide the funding for this endeavor. Instead, Congress passed legislation to reduce the Indians' land base, thereby making it more difficult for them to farm or otherwise develop their economy on the reservation. Agricultural instruction was minimal, schools were inadequate, food rations insufficient, and most Indian agents, who were responsible for carrying out government policies on the reservations, were incompetent or corrupt. Arapaho leaders had to cope with all these problems.

Initially, most of the Northern Arapaho settled in two large camps of tipis, each camp 10 miles apart: Black

Coal's people on the southeast corner of the reservation, where the Wind and Popoagie rivers joined; and Sharp Nose's people on the Little Wind River, to the west of Black Coal's band. A third group, a smaller band led by Friday, also settled on the Little Wind, to the west of Sharp Nose's band.

The Arapaho's strategy for dealing with the problems of subsistence, recognition of their legal right to the reservation, and perpetuation of their cultural heritage was based on their belief in the cycle of the "four hills of life." On the reservation, as in earlier days, the roles of individuals changed as they aged. Along with each of the four hills of life went particular challenges as well as specific responsibilities and privileges. Responsibility for solving problems was undertaken by particular age groups whose members worked together in customary ways. Elders were responsible for religious matters and supervised the middle-aged men who served as leaders in dealings with federal officials, teachers, and missionaries. Youths apprenticed themselves to the older men, taking on responsibilities gradually. Children were raised under the watchful eye of elders, whose prayers the parents still sought.

Indian students at the Episcopal boarding school in Fort Washakie, with missionary Sherman Coolidge standing at far left. The Episcopal school competed with St. Stephens, the Catholic boarding school, for students.

At the Wind River reservation, most babies were born at home, and they were still named by elders to ensure that they would live a good, successful life. Parents continued to invite elders to eat with the family and pray for the child on various occasions. But there were no longer cradles available for all babies, and new cradles were likely to be made of canvas, because deer hide was increasingly difficult to get. Hide clothing, too, was scarce and was worn only on ceremonial occasions. Women continued to make garments embroidered with beads, but they sold much of their work to museums and private collectors for money to buy food and supplies for their families.

As part of the government's "civilization" program, children were forced to attend either the boarding school that had been opened by the government or one run by the Catholic mission on the reservation. At the schools, the children's Indian clothing was taken from them, their long hair cut short, and they were punished for speaking the Arapaho language. Haircutting ceremonies came to replace the ear-piercing rituals of earlier times: A renowned warrior would cut the boy's hair, before a teacher had the chance to do so, and tell of his war exploits; in return he received gifts from the boy's parents.

Games learned at school gradually replaced the older, traditional amusements, but children continued to ride ponies and listen to the stories told by their grandparents. At school, boys and girls were separated and taught different skills. Boys learned to care for livestock and do farm work, girls to sew and do housework. All learned English, the only language they were allowed to speak, and the "three Rs"—reading, writing, and 'rithmetic—that constituted the curriculum in most American schools of the period. Most Arapaho children started school when they were about nine years old and attended school for only three to six years. After leaving school, most began to work and got married. A few went to boarding schools away from the reservation or stayed in school on the reservation to continue their education.

At boarding schools youths were urged to reject Arapaho traditions and were often taught trades, such as tailor, bricklayer, or printer, which could not be practiced on the reservation. The Indian agents gave some young people special privileges and economic aid in an effort to enhance their status and undercut that of the elders, but the youths were ridiculed by their own people if they let an agent influence them.

Later, in 1917, the Episcopal church would open a boarding school in the Arapaho community on the Little Wind River where there were no harsh punishments and children were encouraged to express their Arapaho culture. Federal officials were appalled, but the new school was popular and drew students away from the other two schools on the reservation.

Parents still arranged some marriages for their young adult children,

Members of the 1908 business council delegation to Washington, D.C. Front: Little Wolf, Lone Bear, Yellow Calf; standing, interpreter Tom Crispin.

but gradually most young men and women came to choose their own spouses. The Indian agent or a clergyman performed the ceremony; those who participated in Indian ceremony marriages were put in prison or had their food rations withheld. Although men were now forbidden to have more than one wife, the Arapaho still maintained their customary avoidance and joking relationships with their in-laws.

Young people in their twenties and early thirties were not considered fully mature, particularly because the young men could no longer earn prestige through warfare. Elders recognized that these were frustrating times for young people and tried to respond. They recruited youths into the religious lodges, relaxing the rules for admission and encouraging them to apprentice themselves to older individuals in the ceremonial hierarchy. They allowed young men to move up the age-based ranks much more rapidly than before, offering them a chance for prestige while still perpetuating the age hierarchy. In 1892 the average age of a Spearman had been 30 years; by 1910 it was only 18.

In the early 20th century, the elders helped organize young people into social clubs according to their age and sex. The new organizations, such as a Christmas club and a summer entertainment society, resembled the traditional men's lodges in many ways. These clubs often helped the needy and sponsored community activities. Three singing groups, called drum groups because the singing was accompanied by a large kettle drum, were also organized, and the young men in them were apprenticed to older singers to learn traditional Arapaho songs. These groups sang at social club events.

The clubs, along with religious rituals such as the Offerings Lodge and Pipe ceremonies, gave youths an alternative to the agents' plans and helped to reinforce the authority of the elders. Youths still depended on the elders' guidance and prayers for successful, satisfying lives. When they had difficulties, they often sought a new name from an elder. Old Man Sage told anthropologist Inez Hilger that in 1933 he gave his name to a young man "so that he could go straight."

Mature men in their forties and fifties struggled to make a living while still concentrating on meeting their ritual obligations. This age group included tribal leaders, who had the larger problem of finding ways to help their people.

It was not easy for these men to provide for their families. There were small farm gardens in the large camps, and the men herded livestock communally. Raising livestock was difficult, however, because the Indian agent could not prevent cattle rustling by people who were from off the reservation. Farming was not very productive, because the Arapaho did not have enough money to buy heavy equipment to harvest grain and the federal government was unwilling to assist them. Meanwhile, rations provided by the government became increasingly inadequate. In 1883 the Arapaho received four pounds of beef per person per week; by 1889 the ration had been reduced to one pound. After the turn of the century, the agent was instructed to give rations only to the old and disabled. Often the Arapaho's white neighbors and the agency personnel stole the rations before they could be issued. The resulting deprivation contributed to a high death rate; in 1885 there were 972 Northern Arapaho; in 1893 the population was down to 823. Arapaho men tried to earn money for their families by cutting and selling wood or hauling freight for the agency. Most had gone deeply into debt to the agency trader in order to get food.

To the mature men fell various official and political duties as well. When the Northern Arapaho first settled at Wind River, federal officials still expected to deal with chiefs. The traditional duties of the intermediary chief fell to Black Coal, Sharp Nose, and a

Indian men visiting the Arapahoe Mercantile trading company. People sold surplus crops in order to purchase household goods and farm supplies. From left: *Sumner Black Coal, Thomas Bull Chief, Yellow Plume, William Painted Red, and Old Man Scarface, an Arapaho elder.*

few others who were known to officials by reputation. These leaders not only had outstanding war records but were viewed as levelheaded and generous by their own people. Although these "council chiefs" did not have coercive powers, they were able to influence both their own people and the federal authorities. As participants in the sys-

tem of age-ranked ceremonial lodges, they were subject to the authority of the elders but were also able to call upon the elderly ritual leaders to influence the tribe.

During the early years on the reservation, from about 1878 to 1904, these chiefs had the responsibility of finding solutions to the major problems facing

(continued on page 73)

SYMBOLISM IN SHAPES AND COLORS

The Arapaho put their prayers into everything they made and used. Men generally made their own shields, ceremonial regalia, hunting gear, war equipment, and tools; women made almost everything else the family used, from clothing to carrying bags. Colors and design had religious significance. These symbolic meanings generally depended on the thoughts and inspiration of the individual craftsperson and were not the same for everyone. Many designs are hiiteni, *or life symbols, representing abundance, prosperity, and the life force. The making of some objects, such as tipi ornaments and infants' cradles, was itself a ceremonial act.*

Arapaho artisans saw designs in a dream or spiritual vision in which they might get instructions from a spirit helper to make a particular object. Some designs were handed down from an older person to a younger one. The meanings of the symbols on the objects shown here were explained by the craftspeople to the anthropologist Alfred L. Kroeber, who collected these objects from the Southern Arapaho in 1899 and from the Northern Arapaho in 1900.

A beaded tipi ornament, Southern Arapaho. The concentric arcs represent the whirlwind that was present at the creation of the earth; the sawtooth pattern around the circumference represents human beings. Four narrow black-edged white sectors divide the circular ornament into four larger sectors. Together, the colors red, yellow, black, and white signify the four directions. Four such ornaments were attached around the tipi, with a fifth at the front top. The design and the ceremony in which it was made represent a prayer for a good life, a life in harmony with all of creation.

Girl's buckskin Ghost Dance dress, Southern Arapaho. The designs, seen in a devotee's dream, include the Thunderbird (at center bottom), the buffalo (symbolizing subsistence in the fresh, new world to come), the morning star (whose green edges denote the freshness of that world), and the magpie (a messenger to the spirit world). The black shapes are hiiteni. Other designs include a turtle (symbolic of creation), a cottonwood tree, stars and a new moon (the heavens), a rainbow surrounding a cloud, and a green strip (the rebirth of the earth in springtime). The netted hoop at center suggests a children's game revived in Ghost Dance times.

Ghost Dance feather headdress, Southern Arapaho. It signified the expected return of the dead because spirits seen in visions wore such headdresses.

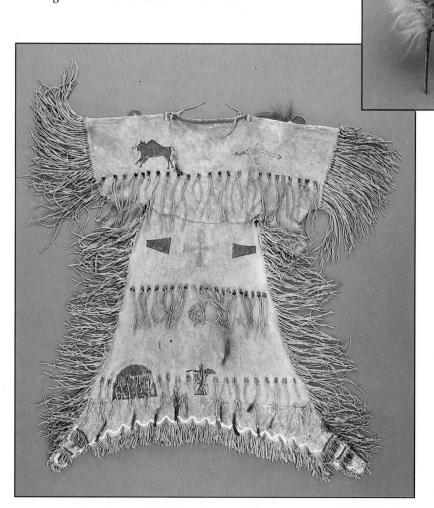

Head ornament worn at peyote
ceremony, Southern Arapaho. The
12 feathers, which represent sticks
in the ceremonial fire, are attached
to knotted leather thongs. The
metal knob represents the sacra-
mental peyote button and the
bead-covered handle the peyote
plant. The blue feathers symbolize
ashes from the ceremonial fire.

Painted sheet with designs seen in a dream, worn as a robe during the Ghost
Dance, Southern Arapaho. The birds are an eagle (right, on the rainbow), a
bull-bat bird (right) and magpie flying across the sky (background), and the
crow messenger (left, on the rainbow), who took the dreamer to a cloud and
related the coming of the new world. The wavy lines carry the birds' voices to
the heavens. Also represented are the morning star (cross) and the earth (red in
lower corners).

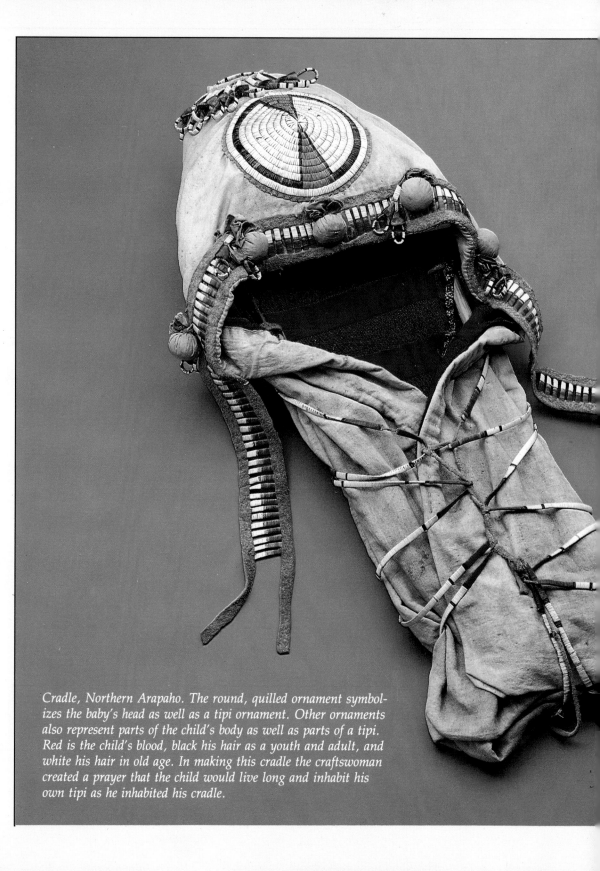

Cradle, Northern Arapaho. The round, quilled ornament symbolizes the baby's head as well as a tipi ornament. Other ornaments
also represent parts of the child's body as well as parts of a tipi.
Red is the child's blood, black his hair as a youth and adult, and
white his hair in old age. In making this cradle the craftswoman
created a prayer that the child would live long and inhabit his
own tipi as he inhabited his cradle.

Child's moccasins, Northern Arapaho. The craftswoman symbolized her prayer that the child's path through life would be safe (avoiding snake bites—the green zigzag beading) and reach old age (to use the sweat house, whose poles and heated stones are represented by the multicolored quillwork).

Girl's leggings and moccasins, Southern Arapaho. The red quill rows are the girl's path through life; the blue beaded triangles are the designs on the rawhide bags she will make. Also shown are hiiteni and animal tracks. The tin rattles frighten snakes.

69

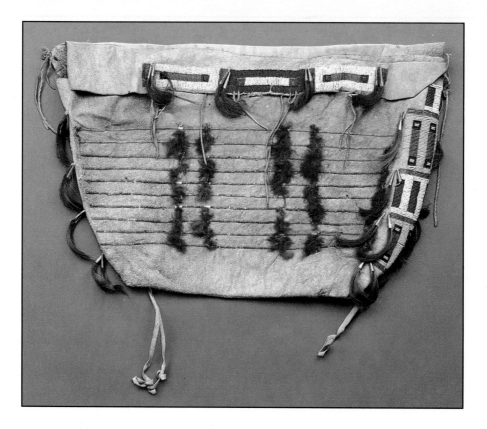

Large, soft hide bag, Southern Arapaho. The quilled stripes represent marks made by tipi poles being dragged when the camp moves. The wool tuft stripes are ravines where camp is set up; the beaded rectangles are hiiteni; the feathers are drying buffalo meat. The bag is a prayer for prosperity.

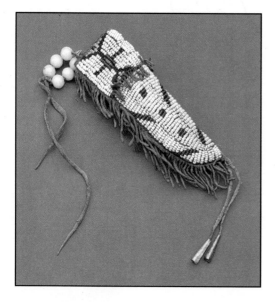

Woman's beaded knife case, Northern Arapaho. The cross at the top represents a person; the triangles above and below it are mountains. The squares below are hiiteni; the wedges that point to them are prayers for desired goals.

Woman's pouch for combs and body paint, Northern Arapaho. The entire beaded design is a wish for prosperity and a good life. Designs represent morning stars (the center crosses), bear claws (the three-pronged shapes), tipis (the pink triangles) separated by trails, and mountain ranges (the border). The designs on the sides at the top are meat-drying racks. On the flap are mountains (triangles) and lakes (squares).

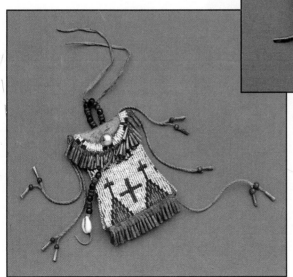

Woman's belt pouch for small items, Northern Arapaho. The overall design is a prayer for prosperity. Symbols include the morning star (the center cross), eagles on tipi poles (crosses on triangles), and meat-drying racks (on the flap).

Parfleche for porcupine quills, Northern Arapaho. The diamond rows represent strings of silver disks worn by prosperous men. Also symbolic of abundance are the colors, which stand for all green, yellow, and red objects, and the unpainted triangles, which are tents.

Parfleche, painted rawhide, Northern Arapaho. The entire design symbolizes the earth and is a prayer for a prosperous, satisfying life. The blue shapes are mountains in whose centers are unpainted valleys, red hills, and a yellow stripe representing a flat plain. The tapering red and yellow areas represent tipis; at their bases, black marks representing tipi pegs bisect unpainted life symbols.

(continued from page 64)

the Arapaho: how to remain permanently at Wind River, how to get enough food to survive, and how to prevent loss of their culture. They set about to convince officials that they were dependable allies who would remain at peace and cooperate with the "civilization" efforts. One of their more dramatic acts toward these ends occurred in 1881, when each Arapaho council chief sent one of his children to the Carlisle Indian School in Pennsylvania. Carlisle was a boarding school with a particularly rigorous program designed to keep all aspects of Indian traditions away from youths of many tribes. The chiefs' children were, in effect, hostages guaranteeing the Arapaho's good conduct. "[We] have given our children, whom we love," said Black Coal to federal officials "into their hands. We wish also to assure you by this that we never more want to go on warpath, but always live in peace."

In their efforts to secure a place for Arapaho on the reservation, the men had to face consistent government efforts to decrease the reservation lands. They cooperated with the agent who, with the consent of Congress, was leasing reservation lands to non-Indian cattle raisers. They would accept individual ownership of land in 1900. More important, by ceding some of their land in 1896 and 1904 they were able to get recognition of the tribe's legal right to the reservation.

The centerpiece of the government's role in reducing reservation lands was shaped by the General Allotment Act,

also known as the Dawes Act, passed by Congress in 1887. This law provided for reservation land to be divided into plots and given, or allotted, to each member of the tribe. Any land left over after all the people on a reservation had received their allotment plots was to be

Two Arapaho youths at the Carlisle Indian School in Carlisle, Pennsylvania. Tribal leaders sent their children to this boarding school as proof of their intent to cooperate with government programs. Carlisle, characterized by rigid discipline and enforced separation of students from their homes, was designed to remove all aspects of the students' Indian culture.

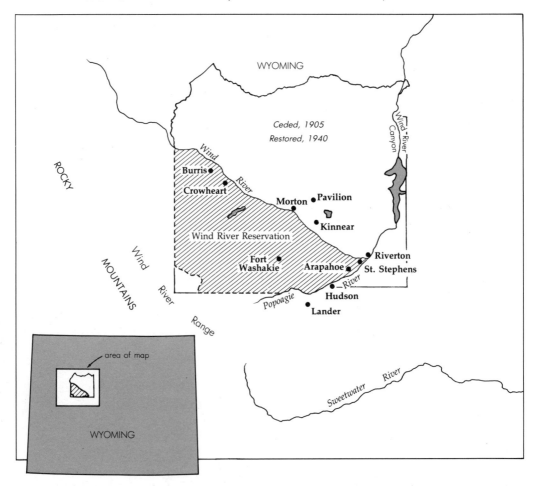

sold to non-Indians, and the income from that sale used for the benefit of the tribe as a whole. The intent was to make inexpensive land available to non-Indians, to end the communal, tribal ownership and use of reservation land, and to make it virtually necessary for Indians to become farmers on their own plots, as other Americans were.

In 1891 and 1894, Congress also passed legislation that allowed both al-lotted plots and unallotted tribally owned land to be leased to non-Indians. These measures were intended to provide income for the Indian people, for Congress was determined to reduce spending on Indian affairs; the measures also served to satisfy the demands of would-be homesteaders for more land. In addition, the legislation specified that a council of tribal leaders should approve the leases; this provision helped to strengthen the Arapaho chiefs. The agent began leasing land to cattle raisers in 1898.

In 1900 the chiefs agreed to allotment, but only on the condition that stone markers be placed to establish Arapaho title to lands on which they had settled. Their allotments were between the forks of the Wind and Popoagie rivers and along the Little Wind River in the vicinity of the largest Arapaho camp there.

At Wind River before allotment, the Shoshone and Arapaho had been pressured to relinquish much of the 2 million acres of reservation land. In 1896 they ceded 10 square miles in the northeast corner of the reservation. After allotment they were pressured to cede more. The Arapaho council chiefs ma-

Northern Arapaho, Shoshone, and U.S. government participants in the treaty council of 1904, at which the Indians were pressured to cede two-thirds of the Wind River reservation. This meeting, however, constituted official recognition of the Arapaho's place at the formerly all-Shoshone site.

A threshing machine and crew on the Wind River reservation. In the 1880s, Arapaho chiefs had large hayfields and vegetable gardens where their followers worked. Later, as in this photograph, men worked in groups on each other's land.

neuvered to keep as much land as possible in tribal ownership and to obtain official recognition of their right to live at Wind River. After the deaths of Black Coal in 1893 and Sharp Nose in 1901, the main Arapaho representative was council chief Lone Bear.

In the cession agreement, signed by the Arapaho as well as the Shoshone in 1904 (but not ratified until 1905), the tribes agreed to cede the lands north of the Big Wind River, about two-thirds of the reservation. The allotted lands were south of the river. In return for the cession each Arapaho received a payment of $50. The government also agreed to establish a subagency at the eastern end of the reservation, which finally constituted the official recognition that se-

cured the Arapaho's place at Wind River.

According to the 1904 agreement with the tribes, the government was to sell the ceded lands and use the proceeds for a per-person payment; irrigation works so that the Shoshone and Arapaho could farm more effectively; and the purchase of cattle, school improvements, and rations. But while payment to the tribespeople was made, the government did not hold to the rest of the terms it had agreed on. The land was not suitable for farming, so homesteaders showed little interest in buying it. Cattle raisers preferred to lease land instead of buying it, so officials continued to lease the north half of the reservation to whites.

To succeed in getting what they wanted, the council chiefs had to unify the Arapaho in support of their positions in order to present a solid front to the Shoshone, who did not want them to receive allotments, and to the federal authorities. The chiefs generated such support in the traditional way, by generosity. In prereservation days, a man wealthy in horses would loan them to others for the hunt, and he would also distribute surplus meat from his own hunting efforts to needy families. On the reservation, the chiefs contributed to their followers' support by distributing food supplies given out by the agents.

Beef rations were delivered to the reservation "on the hoof." When the cattle arrived, the men ran them down and butchered them. The chiefs then distributed the meat. The chiefs received the hides of these slaughtered cows, which they sold, and also got other extra rations—such as up to 100 pounds of flour per week. They used this extra income and food to support needy Arapaho and provide for visitors.

The council chiefs had other reserves to dispense as well. By 1886 Black Coal, Sharp Nose, and other lesser-known council chiefs had large hayfields and vegetable gardens along the rivers, where the Arapaho had constructed irrigation ditches as best they could. The chiefs' followers worked in the fields and shared the produce, and each chief used his own share to support the needy. Sharp Nose, employed

Excavating a canal at Wind River. The government had agreed to give the Indians free water rights but instead charged them fees. Those who could not pay for irrigation water were pressured to lease or sell their land.

Sharp Nose (left) shaking hands with U.S. Army captain William C. Brown at Fort Washakie in 1899. The Arapaho chief was able to use his position as head scout to influence both government officials and fellow Arapaho.

as a scout at nearby Fort Washakie from 1881 to 1890, received scout's rations. He told his commander the amount would be sufficient if he were "selfish enough to use it himself," but instead he used it to "feed all his family and other people depending on him."

Black Coal had another strategy for providing food for his people. He welcomed the Catholic missionaries who came to the reservation in 1884 and helped them select land for gardens. Then he told the priests they would have to move and pay to use other lands; and each time they worked new

land, he asked for a payment. In this way he obtained broken ground—soil ready for planting—for his followers to farm as well as large stores of provisions. The Catholics did not object because they were competing with the Episcopal missionaries who had settled near Sharp Nose's group and were courting the Arapaho. Meanwhile the council chiefs were successfully soliciting provisions from the Episcopal missionaries as well.

There was still another source of revenue over which the council chiefs exercised influence. The reservation lands north of Wind River were leased to non-Indian cattle raisers. The lease money was to be spent by the Indian agent for the benefit of the Indians. Every year the council chiefs told the agent the tribe's consensus as to how the income should be spent—whether it should be used to buy seed, for example, or given to members of the tribe on an individual basis. Because the Bureau of Indian Affairs accepted these recommendations fairly consistently, the Arapaho respected the council chiefs and appreciated their importance. They provided for others and successfully influenced the government to provide support as well.

Black Coal and Sharp Nose were also adept at conveying to their fellow Arapaho the impression that federal officials regarded them highly. Council chiefs went to Washington, D.C., where they received medals and other gifts that symbolized the president's regard. Black Coal had been given a special outfit—a broadcloth suit with a watch and chain—by the secretary of the interior, and he made a point of wearing this on many public occasions. Sharp Nose, who had been General George Crook's head scout in 1876, wore his army uniform; and he also named his son General Crook—a constant reminder to the Arapaho of his army connections.

The chiefs also worked to convince the agent and the missionaries that they were receptive to Christianity and that the Arapaho religion was not a threat to the government's "civilization" program. Chiefs personally welcomed, visited with, and attended the services conducted by missionaries. When the Arapaho had ceremonies, chiefs went to the army commander at Fort Washakie, the military post on the reservation, and assured him the gathering was for peaceful purposes. Although the chiefs had achieved legal status on the reservation in the agreement of 1905, in the years that followed the Arapaho's economic situation deteriorated and repressive measures against their culture continued. The government gradually decreased their rations. Those Arapaho who were employed by the government were usually paid with "purchase orders" that they could redeem only at a particular store, an arrangement that was often abused and resulted in the Indians' being cheated. The government representatives at the land cession council of 1904 had promised to build an irrigation system for the Arapaho and the Shoshone so that they

could get higher yields from their allotment fields. Subsequently the federal government reneged on this agreement and told the Indians that they would have to pay to use water from irrigation ditches the government had built on the reservation. In 1906, Congress passed legislation to allow Indians to sell their allotments. Those without money to pay for irrigation of their farms were pressured by the agent to lease or sell their allotments to non-Indians.

Shortly after 1905, when an irrigation system was completed, most people moved from the three main camps and settled on their allotments in extended family clusters. When they first came to Wind River, they had lived in tipis. Later, unable to replace the worn-out skins used for tipi coverings, they began to live in canvas tents. In the summer they built shelters covered with brush, called "shades," where they cooked, ate, and sometimes slept. On their allotment land they kept gardens and small hay farms. In winter almost everyone moved back to the three large camp communities that still remained—one in the forks of the Wind and Popoagie rivers, one on the lower Little Wind River, and the third on the upper Little Wind.

During the early part of the 20th century, federal officials were no longer swayed by the Arapaho chiefs' reputations for bravery and declarations of peaceful intent. The Arapaho leaders had to change their strategy for dealing with government officials. From about 1906 to 1936 they presented themselves as "progressive" supporters of the government's policy to make Indians self-supporting. In the early 20th century the government encouraged them to elect a representative governing body, called a business council, in place of the chiefs' council. The chiefs agreed, at least outwardly. Now the lease book, which recorded who was leasing tribal land north of the Big Wind and how much income resulted, replaced the medal as a symbol of leadership.

Arapaho leaders made several trips to Washington, D.C., during this period as they tried to improve reservation conditions and gain more control over the reservation's natural resources, such as grazing land and mineral deposits. Money received from leasing land for cattle raising, oil production (which began in 1905), and some mining constituted the tribe's only source of income. Although the business council had the right to approve those who applied to lease their lands, federal officials now spent the lease income without regard for the tribe's wishes. Moreover, the lands were being leased for scandalously low prices. Members of the business council went to Washington in 1908 and 1913, hoping to persuade officials to allow them to set higher prices for leases and to distribute the income to each person in the tribe.

In 1908, delegates from the business council persuaded the government to pay higher wages to Arapaho working on reservation ditches and roads. In 1913, they succeeded in getting the lease fees increased, and they convinced the government to use the lease income to buy the tribe its own cattle herd as well as to build grist- and saw-mills on the reservation. The cattle operation would provide a market for the hay grown by Arapaho farmers, and the mills would ensure fair prices for flour and lumber.

Business council members generally did not act on their own but consulted other Arapaho, particularly elders, before making council decisions. The elders reflected prevailing Arapaho opinion, but they also mobilized public sentiment behind specific goals of their leaders. The most prominent council members and spokesmen were Lone Bear (1854–1920), from the Wind-Popoagie River community, and Yellow Calf (1860–1938), from the Little Wind area. Both were exceptionally articulate in Arapaho and spoke enough English that they were not completely dependent on interpreters. Both had progressed through the men's lodges and served as council chiefs before the business council came into existence. During the 1920s younger men, who had apprenticed themselves to the older council members, began to become prominent.

Council members, like the council chiefs before them, strove to demonstrate generosity to their fellow Arapaho. The Indian agent said of one that he "died in poverty" because of his charity. Until 1917 the council members received sizable quantities of rations and were paid to act as supervisors on

Elderly religious leaders—Samuel Shotgun, Herman Quiver, and Coal Bearing—photographed in the 1920s. Men who had pledged the lodges when they were younger continued to teach traditional rituals and used their influence to gain the people's support for decisions of the business council.

agency work projects. With these supplies and funds they aided the needy, sponsored tribal celebrations, and entertained visitors from other tribes. After 1917 they customarily received gifts of money from the people who leased tribal land, and these funds, too, they contributed to community activities.

Reciprocity held Arapaho social life together. Families helped one another with work, such as haying and building, and shared food and other resources. Those who had paying jobs helped support those who did not. Some federal officials were dismayed that the more affluent and able-bodied Arapaho shared with the poor and weak. This, in their view, was not "progressive"; it was no way for individuals to "get ahead" and "make something of themselves." They were accustomed to people saving their individual earnings and using their accumulated money to advance their own standard of living. Council leader Lone Bear said of these officials: "They do not understand things, and they undertake to think for a man living here. They think their own way and think they can change the Indian in accordance with their own way of living. They think the Indians can make money and have [save] money like they can, but that is impossible." Sharing was the Arapaho way.

The role of elders in coping with reservation problems was no less important than that of middle-aged Arapaho. The elderly religious leaders aided the business council leaders in gaining support from the people, just as they had helped the council chiefs in the past. The ritual leaders often lectured the people in support of farming or other concerns of the leaders. In return, the council members worked diligently to mitigate the Indian agent's efforts to undermine the Arapaho religion. The 1908 delegation, for example, succeeded in convincing federal officials to cease their objections to the Offerings Lodge.

The ritual leaders also conducted ceremonies that helped to unify the people and motivate them to cooperate. The Keeper of the Sacred Pipe, for example, conducted Pipe ceremonies in which an individual vowed to make a prayer-sacrifice to the Pipe. Such vows were made known to the whole tribe, and the vowers were expected to be particularly kind and obliging to others. When there was conflict, ceremonial Grandfathers in the Offerings Lodge could defuse the situation simply by counseling or by pressing a pipe into the hands of a violent individual. The

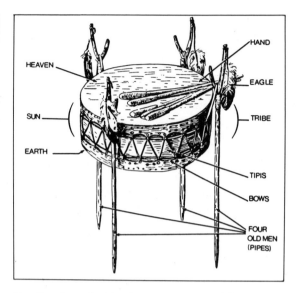

For the Arapaho the drum was a sacred instrument used in ceremonies and to accompany prayer. Each part of the drum traditionally had symbolic significance. In the early 20th century, elders created a drum ceremony to install the people elected to serve on the business council.

person would restrain himself rather than risk supernatural retaliation. Not long after the tribe settled at Wind River, one Arapaho man killed another. In order to preserve the tribe's reputation with federal officials for maintaining peace, the elderly ritual leaders persuaded the murderer to surrender to government authorities. They also dissuaded the victim's relatives from seeking revenge, as had been the custom.

The ritual leaders were generally quite flexible about permitting innovations in customs and ceremonies. In this way changes came about that eased people's adjustment to the new reservation conditions. For example, federal officials had issued orders to the agent to ban the Offerings Lodge ceremony altogether because they objected to some of the forms of sacrifice practiced during the ceremony. To appease these officials, elders in 1890 eliminated the practice of self-torture. This concession made it possible for the lodge itself to continue. After the Arapaho settled on the reservation, the seven Water-Pouring Old Men did not select replacements. Instead, a larger group of knowledgeable elders supervised rituals. Although these ceremonial leaders also had personal medicine power, they did not pass it on to younger men or encourage them to obtain power in a vision quest. Perhaps they felt that such power was too dangerous to entrust to youths who were being educated by non-Indians.

New religions were introduced as well, not only Christianity but observances of Indian origin—the Ghost Dance and peyote ritual—that spread rapidly among Plains Indians in the late 19th and early 20th centuries. Elders allowed the people to participate in new rituals as long as they continued to fulfill their obligations to the Sacred Pipe and kept it first in their hearts. The ritual leaders even worked to accommodate the new religious beliefs and practices while retaining their own religion. The Arapaho were friendly to Christian missionaries and accepted baptism, for example, without renouncing their own religious traditions.

The Ghost Dance ceremony, begun by a Paiute Indian prophet in Nevada named Wovoka, promised the return of the buffalo and of believers' deceased relatives. The Arapaho heard about Wovoka and sent a delegation to learn how to practice the new religion from him. During the ceremony people danced and prayed. Many had visions of the better life to come. The Ghost Dance movement flourished from 1889 to the early 1890s. After that it was gradually modified into another ceremony, the Crow Dance ritual. An individual would vow to sponsor the Crow Dance ceremony as part of a prayer. In this way the new ceremony was more like the traditional lodge system. The Crow Dance was particularly popular among young people because it offered an opportunity for them to earn prestige.

In the peyote ceremony, people ingest the peyote cactus, which has hallucinogenic properties, as part of an all-night prayer service. The peyote appears to enhance the sensation of being in communication with the supernatural. Peyote had long been used by the Indians of Mexico and the southwest to enhance religious experiences. It was introduced to the Wind River Arapaho by youths who learned the ritual while visiting the Southern Arapaho in Oklahoma in the late 1890s.

The ritual authorities also found a way to use the business council to perpetuate their own influence and frustrate the Indian agents' efforts to undermine their authority. When it came time to elect the members of the

Northern Arapaho and Shoshone members of Wind River's Joint Tribal Council, 1938. Among them is Arapaho member Nellie Scott, one of the first women to serve in this position.

council, the elders chose the men and then installed them in office with a specially created drum ceremony. The singers brought the drum to the center of the camp. As they sang, the elders danced with great dignity around the drum with the men they had chosen. The drum was a sacred symbol. It was painted red, symbolizing old age and the elders' role as intermediaries between the people and the Creator. The sound of the drum, the eagle feathers attached to it, and other symbols used in the ceremony represented the passage through the division between earth and sky, between the people and the Creator. The songs of the drum group were prayers for assistance in the difficult tasks ahead. The drum ceremony validated the leadership positions of the council members and helped generate support for them from the people. At the same time, the ceremony inspired council members to work on behalf of the people and to accept the guidance of the elders. The prayers of the elders were as necessary in reservation life as they had been in buffalo-hunting times. After the drum ceremony, the new council members and their families held a feast and gave away property to the crowd. Then the results of the "election" were reported to the Indian agent.

In 1930 the federal government insisted that council members be elected by ballot. Even then, elders retained considerable influence over the selection process by expressing their support of certain candidates. The first people elected by ballot were those who had been chosen to serve on the council before 1930. Later younger men, often World War II (1941–45) veterans, were elected. Following elections, elders installed the new council members with the drum ceremony, and those elected accepted the authority of the elders just as those appointed earlier had. Elected council members were also expected to pursue the goals of their constituents, as the appointed leaders had in the past.

The elders remained flexible about innovations. They created, for example, new positions of responsibility for rit-

Arapaho women working in a canning factory at Wind River in 1935. The cannery was built with federal funding as part of the program known as the Indian New Deal.

uals, which gave ceremonial authority to more people. They also divided the responsibilities of people in different authority positions as a way of limiting the growing powers of the council. The business council, for example, managed relations with non-Indians. The elderly ritual leaders did not serve on the council; they directed religious life. Thus the elders were not vulnerable to criticism from people who were annoyed with a decision made by the council. A Dance Committee supervised club activities; the committee was composed of elders and their younger apprentices, who were chosen by the elders before 1951 but were elected thereafter.

Helen Cedartree outside her home at Wind River. By the early 1940s, about two-thirds of the tribe lived in single- or multiple-room log or wood-frame houses. The rest, however, continued to live in canvas tents.

The elders were also intimately involved in the Arapaho's continuing struggle to obtain control of reservation resources. Their involvement was made possible by new federal policies toward Indians begun in 1934, during the first term of President Franklin Roosevelt. With John Collier as commissioner of Indian affairs, the programs known as the Indian New Deal constituted a complete reorganization of the relationship between Indians and the federal government. Many tribes now were able to form their own governing bodies that would have increased their jurisdiction over reservation affairs. The federal government also took steps to protect land already owned by tribes and to hear Indian claims concerning rights to natural resources, including land and water, and for payment still due on previous land cessions. There was at last a favorable climate for remedying the wrongs done to Indians in past years.

The people at the Wind River reservation, Shoshone as well as Arapaho, moved quickly to take advantage of the new policies. In 1927 Congress had passed legislation to allow the Shoshone to file a suit in the court of claims for damages against the United States for locating the Arapaho on the Shoshone Reservation in violation of the Shoshone's treaty. When the Shoshone won their suit in 1937, the Arapaho benefited also. The reservation's name was changed from Shoshone to Wind River, and a portion of the monetary award was used to buy more land for both

tribes. The Shoshone were awarded more than $4 million, $1 million of which Congress decreed would be used to purchase land. In 1940, at the discretion of Congress, the portions of the reservation that had been ceded in 1905 but not sold were restored to the tribes by the secretary of the interior, and much of the land owned by non-Indians was purchased from them by the tribes. In a plan worked out in Congress, the Arapaho borrowed $500,000 from the Shoshone, who used the remainder of their land-purchase fund, and both tribes bought these lands. Thus, reservation resources were greatly expanded.

The business councils of both tribes then began a campaign to bring about increased production from oil wells on these lands. Federal authorities had not adequately supervised the companies that leased oil-rich Wind River land. Because the companies were not required to do test drillings, because they sometimes capped wells instead of continuing to produce from them, and because officials had not prevented sales and subleases to speculators, the tribes had lost a considerable amount of potential income over the years. The Arapaho and Shoshone councils sent delegations to Washington to convince the secretary of the interior to authorize increased production. In 1939 the Wind River delegates accomplished their goal.

Next the two business councils fought the Department of the Interior for the right to obtain per-person payments of the income due to both tribes. Up to this time, at Congress's direction, the income from royalties from oil and leases on tribal land had gone into the U.S. Treasury, where it was administered by the secretary of the interior on behalf of the Shoshone and Arapaho. The secretary had directed that the money be spent to improve agency buildings, pay salaries of non-Indian agency employees, and for other purposes of which the tribes did not necessarily approve. He had opposed giving the money directly to Indian families, saying they would not spend it wisely. The business councils wanted the money to go to the people because there was great poverty at Wind River. All Arapaho households needed money to pay for food, health care, and other needs. In 1936 the Arapaho population was 1,128, more than twice what it had been at the turn of the century. This rapid growth was stretching meager resources to the limit. Housing was inadequate: A 1940 survey of 218 Arapaho households by the Bureau of Indian Affairs showed about a third still living in tents, another third in single-room log houses, and a final third in log or frame houses with two rooms or more. There were serious health problems such as tuberculosis. All but 10 Arapaho families were receiving some form of financial support from government relief programs.

In 1947 a delegation from the Arapaho and Shoshone business councils appeared before Congress. To influence legislators, they referred to the number of men from Wind River who had been in military service during World War II and to the many injustices the tribes had suffered under federal supervision. The delegation succeeded in convincing Congress to allow two-thirds of the tribal income to be distributed in regular per-person payments. In 1956 the proportion allocated for individual payments was increased to 85 percent of tribal income. The remaining 15 percent was to be administered by the business council and spent primarily on helping the needy, for legal fees incurred in defending tribal interests, and to pay the operating expenses of the tribal government.

After the Arapaho began to receive individual payments, their living standards improved tremendously. Between 1947 and 1951, 87 new homes were built, most households installed electricity, and most families no longer had to rely on relief monies.

In 1946, Congress established the Indian Claims Commission (ICC) to rule on charges brought by Indian groups who argued that they had not received adequate payment when their land was sold or that their property, including mineral and other resources, had been mismanaged. In 1955 the combined Northern and Southern Arapaho divisions, together with the Cheyenne, filed a claim with the ICC for violation of the 1851 treaty of Horse Creek and for inadequate compensation for land subsequently taken from them. They won the case in 1961 and were awarded a multimillion-dollar judgment. The Northern Arapaho business council and the tribal elders, who had worked jointly on the case, gained considerable prestige; the authority of both was validated by the lawsuit's success. In the 20th century, the Northern Arapaho not only maintained continuity with their past in a very important way but also accomplished practical goals that improved their lives. ▲

Southern Arapaho chief Left Hand and son Grant, in school uniform, at the Carlisle Indian School.

ASSIMILATION TESTED:
THE SOUTHERN ARAPAHO,

1871–1964

The Southern Arapaho numbered about 1,650 when they all finally settled, with the Cheyenne, at Darlington Agency on the North Canadian River in 1871. In many ways their experience in Indian Territory (Oklahoma) resembled that of their northern kin; in important ways it was different. The Southern Arapaho, for example, had an adequate food supply for a number of years. Some buffalo still roamed the reservation and its vicinity, and the tribe separated into several bands to hunt them in late fall and again in summer. After these hunts they returned to the agency, where Indian agent Brinton Darlington had planted corn, melons, and garden vegetables that the Arapaho assumed were theirs to take. The agency was staffed by members of the Society of Friends, or Quakers, who sought to teach the Indians farming and cattle raising through example rather than by force. The Arapaho chiefs tried to oblige Darlington, whom they liked, and they quickly learned to plant and supervise work on small patches of corn and melons.

As with the Northern Arapaho, however, many cultural traditions endured in the first two decades of reservation life. Women continued to give birth at home, and the parents sponsored feasts to name their infant and to announce its first successful attempt to walk. Boys practiced hunting with small bows and arrows, and girls played with toy tipis and learned to dress and decorate hides. A boarding school was established at the agency, but parents were reluctant to let their children live there, especially since the school quickly became known for having a high death rate due to malaria and to other illnesses that stemmed from an inadequate sewage-disposal system. For some time the agent was able to recruit only orphans to attend classes. Mennonite missionaries (a Swiss-Dutch Protestant sect) also established a school at Darlington, and another at Cantonment (now called Canton), 50 miles northwest at the site of a former army garrison, but these schools also failed to attract students. Parents resented the schools' practices of cutting the children's hair and forcing them to give up their good buckskin clothing for school uniforms. The children were not used to following schedules, so that a teacher had to walk through the camps blowing a cow horn to summon them to class.

In 1879 Southern Arapaho chief Little Raven, his successor Left Hand (no relation to the Left Hand killed at Sand Creek), and other chiefs who were heads of the Arapaho bands decided to send their children to the Carlisle Indian School in Pennsylvania. Like their Northern Arapaho contemporaries, they hoped to prove their loyalty to the United States. Following their example, other parents gradually began to send their children to one of the three reservation schools. There the boys learned how to raise crops and herd cattle, and the girls to sew and make clothing from cloth distributed to families every year. (In the Medicine Lodge Treaty of 1867, the federal government had guaranteed to distribute clothing, household utensils, and other goods to the Arapaho and Cheyenne for 25 years, or until 1892.) Children were paid for their work at the agency school. Their parents could take them out of school to participate in ceremonies, such as the Offerings Lodge. The Mennonites sent about 20 Arapaho children every year to Halstead, Kansas, where they all lived on a farm with a Mennonite family, learning English (and some German, since most Mennonites were of German origin) and farming methods. By 1890 most Ara-

paho children had at least a rudimentary knowledge of English.

Marriages were still arranged or, if they resulted from a courtship, approved by the bride's and groom's families with an exchange of gifts, which usually included horses. As at Wind River, the men seldom had more than one wife, primarily because one wife could now manage the household tasks; there were, for example, fewer hides to be tanned than in buffalo-hunting days. Pressure from the Indian agent also influenced Arapaho men to give up polygyny.

With the buffalo nearly extinct by this time, men hunted deer, quail, turkey, and prairie chicken to supplement the weekly beef ration, which was enough to last only about four days. A family that could not afford food or find game would have little but water for the remaining three days. So men worked at what jobs they could find to earn cash and did their best to grow corn in a region where recurrent droughts and other factors made farming unreliable. A few cared for small herds of cattle, and most sold wood and hauled freight for the agency. Some men were hired at the agency as herders, blacksmiths, or police. A few women also worked at the government school in domestic jobs. The yearly distribution of cloth and clothing helped substitute for the scarcity of hides. The men wore cloth shirts with their breechcloths, leggings, and moccasins. The men were still more comfortable in their

A bead-embroidered pouch made especially to hold the ration tickets that enable a family to receive flour, beef, and other essentials.

traditional clothing, and those who received trousers would often cut out the seat and use them as leggings. Men still spent much time repairing ceremonial equipment and making bows and arrows.

Women now made their tipi covers out of the yearly issue of canvas and made dresses and leggings from this cloth as well. Some families began living in tent-houses instead of tipis. These were built by stretching canvas over a wooden house frame. Missionary women taught many Arapaho how to use a sewing machine. Women carried the family's ration tickets in a pouch made just for that purpose. The tickets determined the amount of flour and other food the family received on issue day. It was the responsibility of the women to cut the beef into strips and dry it in the sun and wind so that it did not spoil. Women also continued to gather wood and wild plants. They cooked cattail roots in stews and dried wild grapes, cherries, and roses. The women tanned cowhide and sold the hides to traders to get cash. Gradually they began to purchase bedsteads, tables, and stoves for their tipis or tent-houses.

The Southern Arapaho's middle-aged leaders still played an important role in the 1870s. Band headmen took responsibility for overseeing the weekly distribution of beef to their people. The agency staff let a steer out of the corral and each headman directed the men of his band in running the animal down, butchering it, and then distributing the meat. Headmen and chiefs got extra rations and goods, which they used to support needy band members. Before the railroad reached Darlington, the agency hired the bands to transport, by wagon train, the supplies needed at the agency. The band headman was the leader of his band's freight train; and the freighting jobs were rotated among the bands. The men's lodge societies continued to exist, functioning to maintain order in the camps.

The Arapaho leaders' goal during this early reservation period was to convince the government to separate them

The weekly beef distribution at Darlington agency, 1890. Under the supervision of the agency staff, cattle held in issue pens were killed and butchered by the Arapaho.

from the Cheyenne, which they hoped to achieve by cooperating with government officials and programs. In contrast to the Cheyenne, who had sporadic violent confrontations with non-Indians and who went to war again in 1873–74, the Arapaho protected the agency and escorted army troops through dangerous country. They became accustomed to demanding "gifts" from the whites in return for their services—and they usually got what they asked. John Seger, an agency employee, remarked, "We learned to trust the Arapahos and yet some of them, as they saw how much we depended upon them, be-

came very exacting and expected a great many privileges. They took the liberty of entering employees' houses whenever they chose to do so, and were often annoying. They felt we owed them a great deal—and we did."

The Arapaho went out of their way to cooperate with the government's agricultural program. They would break the soil with butcher knives when promised farm equipment did not arrive in time. They struggled to build up herds despite constant thefts of Indian livestock by non-Indian desperadoes in what was still only the unsettled frontier of the United States.

Because goverment officials considered houses more "civilized" than tipis, they pressed some Arapaho to move into them, even though the tipis were often better insulated and more comfortable. Important chiefs agreed to accept houses, and some even paid to have them constructed. Little Raven accepted the abandoned hospital building at Cantonment and, although he continued to spend most of his time in his tipi, he planted 40 acres of corn there. After a house was built for the chief Big Mouth, he pointed out that the house had only four rooms and he had seven wives, each of whom demanded a room for herself. He decided to move his camp close to the house and to store his hides and keep his dogs in it.

The Southern Arapaho leaders' efforts resulted in an agreement in 1873 between a delegation of their chiefs and the secretary of the interior to establish separate reservations for the Southern Cheyenne and Southern Arapaho, but Congress never approved the agreement. Arapaho leaders kept trying until their reservation was abolished in 1890.

The elders continued to fulfill their traditional responsibilities; they conducted the lodge ceremonies and the Sun Dance and they continued to instruct and encourage their juniors. Elderly men who had supernatural power to cure tried to heal their people, who had been made sick from water polluted by wastes from a nearby army post and malaria transmitted by swarms of mosquitoes that infested the area.

Meanwhile, rationing was slowly phased out, as it had been at Wind River. By 1883, Brinton Darlington's successor as agent, John Miles, began to lease reservation grazing land to non-Indian cattle raisers and distribute the "resulting grass money" income to the Arapaho and Cheyenne twice a year. In 1885, however, Cheyenne opposition moved President Grover Cleveland to eject the cattle raisers. Shortly afterward the surrounding non-Indian population began to put pressure on the government to abolish Darlington's reservation status and open its land for settlement.

In 1889 the Southern Arapaho learned of a prophet far to the west who had learned in a vision how the Indians could bring back the lost buffalo herds and their former way of life. The Arapaho were desperate. Their numbers had been reduced, primarily by deaths from malaria, to 1,137. The United States had kept none of the promises made in the Medicine Lodge Treaty of 1867.

Hearing that the Northern Arapaho were already practicing the Ghost Dance, Black Coyote went to Wind River to learn about the ritual. Smithsonian Institution ethnologist James Mooney, who studied the Ghost Dance extensively, described Black Coyote as "a man of contemplative disposition, much given to speculation on the unseen world." Black Coyote was intensely religious. When he was a young man, several of his children had died. As he prayed for the health of his remaining children he had a vision in which he was instructed to cut 70 pieces of skin from his upper body as a sacrifice to accompany his prayers. He completed the sacrifice, and the rest of his children survived.

Black Coyote returned to his people from Wyoming in the spring of 1890 and began to lead Ghost Dance ceremonies. In the fall, Sitting Bull, a Southern Arapaho who had been living with the Northern division, arrived at Darlington and began to lead the devotees. Sitting Bull was able to hypnotize people into a trance by the use of a feather. In their trance state they saw their deceased relatives in another, better world where Arapaho hunted buffalo again and prospered in their traditional ways. People danced with feathers of the crow, eagle, or magpie. They wore painted designs representing these birds or the mythological Thunderbird, which caused thunder and lightning, or of other celestial objects that appeared to them in trances. The wings of the birds, messengers from the supernatural world above, would help symbolically to carry the devotee upward to facilitate a trance.

Parents, desperate to see their deceased children, joined the new religion by the hundreds. The Ghost Dance also encouraged the revival of handcrafts and the perpetuation of the Sun Dance and prayer with the Sacred Pipe. Southern Arapaho continued to make pilgrimages north to Wyoming to pray with the Pipe. Through faithful performance of the Ghost Dance, devotees

Arapaho women in a trance during Ghost Dance rites. This photograph was taken in about 1893 by the ethnologist James Mooney.

could hasten the replacement of the world they now knew with the one they saw in their visions.

While the Arapaho had been learning the Ghost Dance, events were taking place that would make their situation even more grave. Indian lands were coveted by would-be settlers. As a result, Congress in 1887 passed the General Allotment Act, which affected all reservations. Officials began to plan the divison of the reservations into small sections that would be given, or allotted, to individuals. Land that remained unallotted was to be sold to non-Indians. In October 1890, a commission came to negotiate with the Cheyenne and the Arapaho for the allotment of the reservation and the sale of "surplus" land. The Indians were shocked and dismayed. They had been

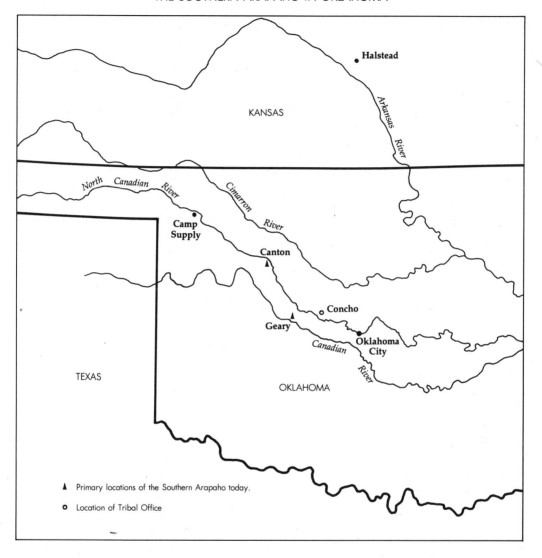

KANSAS

Halstead

Arkansas River

North Canadian River

Cimarron River

Camp Supply

Canton

Concho

Geary

Oklahoma City

Canadian River

TEXAS

OKLAHOMA

▲ Primary locations of the Southern Arapaho today.

o Location of Tribal Office

promised possession of their lands for as long as they wanted them. They knew that their only hope of becoming fully self-sufficient was to raise cattle and that they needed all of the reservation land to support a cattle business. Now they were being forced to accept the breakup of the reservation and the loss of land on which their very survival depended. The government commission presented them with a document in which they had to agree to the cession of much of the reservation. Officials threatened them with the complete cutoff of rations, bribed their interpreters, promised them they would be supported in grand style, and forged many signatures on the cession agreement. Despite evidence of fraud, Congress approved the cession on March 3, 1891.

Principal spokesman Left Hand (who succeeded Little Raven, who died in 1889) and other chiefs had meanwhile become converts to the Ghost Dance religion. Now, faced with the threat of cession, Left Hand asked Sitting Bull for advice. Sitting Bull believed the message of Wovoka—that a new world was coming very soon. The troublesome white people would be barred from this world, and all would be as it was before they came. He told Left Hand to sign the agreement but to obtain the best terms for the tribe that he could. Despite bitter opposition from many Cheyenne, Left Hand and the other Arapaho leaders agreed to the

cession. They did, however, struggle to obtain larger allotments and more money as compensation to the tribes.

As he signed, Left Hand said, "I see the new land coming." Even after the prophecy failed to materialize, many Arapaho continued to dance for several years, for they believed the Ghost Dance ritual would prevent sickness and would lead to a better life sometime in the future. By the 1920s, however, the Ghost Dance served primarily a social rather than religious purpose.

After the cession of 1891, the lands of the Cheyenne and the Arapaho were opened for settlement by non-Indians. The original reservation had been about 4 million acres. Each Cheyenne and Arapaho was allotted 160 acres. These allotments, totaling a little over half a million acres, were then put into trust

Homesteaders in Dewey County, Oklahoma, in 1892, shortly after the 3½ million acres of Southern Arapaho and Cheyenne land ceded by the Indians was opened for non-Indian settlement.

status. This meant that they were controlled by federal officials on behalf of the Indians and for 25 years they could not be sold or taxed by the Oklahoma Territory. The remaining 3½ million acres were opened for settlement by non-Indians. In compensation, the federal government agreed to pay the tribes $1.5 million dollars, or about 40 cents an acre. Of this amount, the tribes were to receive $500,000 paid in equal amounts to each person; in actuality they received less. The remaining $1 million was placed in the U.S. Treasury to earn 5 percent annual interest. The tribes were to receive the interest each year in payments that amounted to less than $20 per person.

The land allotted to the Southern Arapaho was mostly in blocks along the lower Canadian and North Canadian rivers. On April 19, 1892, the remainder of the reservation land was opened for homesteading. About 30,000 settlers streamed onto the former reservation lands. The area was organized into six counties, and several towns were built. Now the Indians constituted only 10 percent of the population.

With allotment came a new government effort to compel the Indians to assimilate, to adopt a style of life like that of their non-Indian neighbors. The assimilation policy assumed that if Indians were given very little economic assistance and forced to live on small family farms side by side with white farmers, they would see the superiority of their white neighbors' way of life and voluntarily change their own.

In 1895 the agent issued beef that had already been butchered to each head of household. This was an effort to undercut the authority of Arapaho leaders, who had previously held responsibility for distributing the beef ration to their followers. The agent ordered that no camps should contain more than four families, that the Arapaho were not to visit other families, that they were not to hold any assemblies or dances, Indian-custom marriages, or religious rituals, and they were not to share provisions. Failure to abide by these rules would result in a family's loss of rations or possibly a jail term. The Arapaho were stunned; the cession agreement that they had signed had promised rations and payments without setting any conditions.

To deflect the opposition of the Indian agents, Arapaho leaders adopted a strategy of placating them. The Cheyenne were openly resisting the agents' policies, so the Arapaho's apparent cooperation won them some concessions. Left Hand and other chiefs openly showed support for the schools and routinely visited them to encourage the students. In 1895 Left Hand consented to have a minister officiate at his daughter's marriage, which the agent believed set a good example for the other Indians. While the Cheyenne met resistance at every turn, Arapaho leaders convinced agents to permit their Offerings Lodge on several occasions. To get acceptance for the ceremony they described it as an innocent-sounding "willow dance" on one occasion and a

The 1899 Southern Arapaho and Cheyenne delegation sent to Washington, D.C. Black Coyote is standing at far left in the second row.

ceremony to pray for the crops at another. Later, during World War I, they would conceal the Offerings Lodge ceremony as a "patriotic dance" or a "Red Cross Dance." Embarrassed federal officials could hardly refuse the Arapaho permission to gather, ostensibly to raise money and pray for the war effort. They held other traditional dances under the guise of Christmas, Thanksgiving, or Fourth of July celebrations or as part of agricultural fairs.

This strategy of accommodation rather than confrontation was designed to get other concessions from federal officials as well. On one occasion, in 1898, the Arapaho were allowed to send a delegation of chiefs to Washington even though the Cheyenne were refused permission. The delegation succeeded in gaining more rations and more agency jobs for both the Cheyenne and the Arapaho. In later years other delegations repeatedly pressured officials not to abolish the trust status of Indian-owned land, which would subject the already exploited people to taxation.

The loss of the reservation combined with the assimilation policy brought increased poverty to the Southern Arapaho and the Cheyenne. The problems encountered by the Northern Arapaho during the reservation era pale in comparison. In the 1890s the very lives of the Southern Arapaho were at risk, for some of their white neighbors felt no compunction about shooting them on sight. Between 1892 and 1901, the Southern Arapaho and Southern Cheyenne lost most of the property that they had managed to accumulate. Their white neighbors, many of whom had been poorer than the Indians when they arrived in 1892, trespassed on Indian allotments at will, stealing timber, tools, saddles, posts, wire, and, most significantly, livestock. Settlers who leased Indian land often stole the Indians' property and frequently failed to pay their rent. Crimes against Indians were ignored by territory officials. Gradually the Indians became poorer and the whites more prosperous.

In the towns merchants prospered at the expense of the Indians. They loaned money to Indians at exorbitant interest rates, with property as collateral. When an Indian fell behind on repayments, the lenders seized property that was worth far more than the amount of the loan. The merchants charged Indians excessively high prices and encouraged them to buy on time.

An 1888 photograph shows one of the trading stores at Darlington Agency. Merchants prospered at the expense of the Southern Arapaho. When the Indians could not repay the high interest on loans, storekeepers claimed the property that had been pledged as collateral.

As soon as the Indians missed a payment, the merchants repossessed their merchandise.

In the early 20th century, it became obvious to federal officials that the measures intended to force assimilation had failed to eradicate Arapaho traditions. Harsher measures were instituted. Rations were stopped. Officials were determined that every man would farm or starve, but crop yields in this part of Oklahoma were too low to support even efficient, experienced white farmers on land similar to that of the Indians. The Arapaho had no choice but to depend on the small per capita payment they received from the government and the money that they got from leasing the portion of their land that they could not farm. Officials, eager to gratify non-Indians clamoring for land, determined that leasing was a sign of laziness and started to encourage Indians to sell their land instead.

In 1902, Congress set aside the 1892 agreement and passed the Dead Indian Land Act, which allowed Cheyenne and Arapaho heirs to sell the allotments they had inherited from deceased relatives. This was legally necessary in order to remove the land from the trust status provided for in the 1891 cession

An Arapaho camp near Fort Reno, Oklahoma, around 1905. Even after allotment, many Arapaho families chose to live in large camps, maintaining stability and a sense of community.

agreement. The 1902 act precipitated massive fraud; the agent was unable to protect the interests of the Indians, who generally were paid less than the land was worth.

In 1906 Congress passed the Burke Act, which allowed the secretary of the interior to declare Indians "competent" to receive a fee patent, or legal proof of ownership, on their allotment so that they could sell it. Again Indians were cheated. Persons incapable of understanding the transactions were not prevented from selling their land below market value. As historian Donald Berthrong observed in 1975, even the government's own investigation—initiated after charges of corruption—concluded that the new legislation brought "joys to the grafter and confidence man and abject poverty to the Indian."

Pressure from settlers for Indian land increased. Officials in Washington responded in 1917 by declaring even more Arapaho and Cheyenne competent to manage their own affairs—and to sell their land. A fourth-grade education in a government vocational school was considered proof of competency. By 1920 more than half of the allotments had been sold; by 1928, 63 percent were no longer owned by the Indians. Most families retained one member's land to live on or lease and gradually sold off the land of other family members.

The opening of the reservation resulted not only in the impoverishment of the Southern Arapaho; it also threatened their existence as a distinct com-

munity that had its own ways of maintaining order and organizing people to work together and help one another. The contrast with the Northern Arapaho is striking. Their leaders were able to obtain greater control over tribal resources. As they gradually succeeded in this, they retained their people's respect. The Southern Arapaho, on the other hand, had no tribal resources left, and so their leaders had little hope of improving the people's situation. By the 1930s they were no longer able to provide for needy families. Since leadership was associated with generosity, the Southern Arapaho leaders gradually lost their people's confidence between 1892 and 1937.

The assimilation policies threatened to undermine the Arapaho's relationship with the Creator as well, for the agents attempted to prevent them from holding religious rituals. Chiefs were able, however, to prevent a ban on ceremonies, and they supported periodic gatherings that helped promote tribal unity and a sense of community.

Even after allotment, Arapaho families still lived on the allotments of a band leader or a senior family member for a few months and in the large camps for the rest of the year. School-age children were sent away to the government boarding schools at Cantonment or Darlington. They were allowed to return to their families for Christmas, when the Arapaho gathered in one large camp (or, in the 1920s, two large camps, one near Canton and the other near Geary) and had dances and other entertainments. Children also returned to camp in the summer. In the fall, just before they went back to school, the tribe had a dance at which parents gave away what property they could—a blanket, a horse—to honor their children. In the 20th century the haircutting ritual had become unnecessary, because children and youths were used to having short hair; now the dance was the parents' way of preparing their children for school. Dances were also held during the two world wars for Arapaho soldiers.

Despite the assimilation policy, Arapaho of all ages retained a distinct cultural identity. Young people continued to marry with the customary exchange of gifts. Later, after the relationship appeared to be secure, a couple would also complete a legal ceremony. In-law avoidance and joking relationships persisted. Most married couples had to live on the allotment of a parent. By the 1920s, young people who had been born after the 1892 allotment had no land of their own. Young men who had been trained in agricultural work at school helped their fathers or fathers-in-law farm. Those youths who had attended eastern boarding schools such as Carlisle had generally learned trades that they could not practice when they returned. Many worked at the agency as clerks or in some other capacity. Several of these youths, who formed a kind of elite group because they were better educated than most Arapaho, soon became disillusioned with the value of assimilating and returned to Arapaho

traditional practices and beliefs. Some became regular participants in the Offerings Lodge, which continued to be vowed regularly until the early 1930s. Increasingly they became devotees of the peyote ritual, which had been introduced in the 1890s. By the 1920s, when they were of middle age, they were leaders in the peyote religion. Older leaders also relied on this group to serve as interpreters.

After receiving allotments, middle-aged men farmed a few acres, helping one another by sharing farm equipment and pooling their labor. In order to buy food and supplies for their families, they relied on credit extended by the stores in the area, which charged inflated prices. In exchange for money, the men put up their tools, farm equipment, livestock, and eventually their land as collateral. Sometimes they could not pay all of their bills and the merchants foreclosed. Women made a significant contribution to the income of the household with the money they received from leasing or selling their allotment lands. Federal regulations allowed women to inherit equally with their brothers, so a woman could own as much as or more land than the men in her family. By the 1920s, however, there was little land left to farm or lease.

By the 1920s most Arapaho lived in houses. These were often built with the women's income and thus were considered the women's property, as the tipis had been. Families survived by community-wide sharing. Elders, who were likely to have inherited many allot-

Members of the 1956 Cheyenne-Arapaho business committee. The agency superintendent is in the front row at left.

ments, were important contributors to the households of their children. People who helped the needy were held in high regard. Elders also put considerable time into fulfilling their ritual responsibilities.

There was much sickness. The scarcity and poor quality of food and shelter made people readily susceptible to contagious diseases. Tuberculosis was especially widespread. The Arapaho population continued to decline: In 1900 there had been 981 Southern Arapaho; in 1929, there were only 820.

In these times of adversity, the Arapaho relied on religion. At the turn of the century, virtually all Arapaho sought aid from the Creator through Offerings Lodge vows or other vows to sacrifice property to the Sacred Wheel. The Wheel was carried during the dancing in the Offerings Lodge by the individual who had vowed to sponsor the ceremony. Southern Arapaho often made prayer-sacrifices by donating property to the Wheel, as the Northern Arapaho in Wyoming did for the Sacred Pipe kept there. The Wheel, other ar-

Participants rest in the morning after holding an all-night peyote ceremony in the tipi. This photograph was taken in 1912 in Clinton, Oklahoma.

ticles used in the Offerings Lodge, and the Offerings Lodge itself symbolized the events of creation in Arapaho mythology. Each of the age-graded men's societies had a role in conducting the Offerings Lodge. Many men contributed time, money, and property, as society members and all men helped their relatives and friends to fulfill their ritual responsibilities. By the 1920s those who had been middle-aged participants at the turn of the century were elders helping to direct the rite. In the 1920s some young men participated; others were respectful but more committed to peyote ceremonies.

The peyote rite was introduced to the Southern Arapaho in the 1890s by individuals in the tribe who had participated in the peyote ceremonies of the Kiowa Indians. Participants stayed up all night fasting, singing religious songs, and praying while ingesting the peyote cactus, which has hallucinogenic properties, and following a ritual prescribed by the leader of the ceremony. Praying in the peyote ceremony was similar in many respects to more traditional ways of praying. Participants might receive a vision offering guidance and reassurance. The peyote served as a medium of prayer, as did the Sacred Pipe or Wheel. The peyote ceremony served as a prayer-sacrifice, usually made to help someone recover from illness. Ceremonies were held after an individual vowed to the Creator to bear the expenses of the rite. The peyote rite allowed for a wide range of underlying beliefs and various interpretations of its symbols. Prayers could be made to the Great Mystery Above, God, the Creator, or Jesus Christ. Songs often focused on sacred birds as messengers to and from the supernatural world above; some participants believed that the birds were imbued with supernatural power; others thought that they symbolized angels.

In 1934 the Roosevelt administration began to sponsor legislation that made major reforms in federal Indian policy. The Oklahoma Indian Welfare Act was passed in 1937, and officials assured the Cheyenne and the Arapaho that the remaining Indian-owned lands would remain in trust status indefinitely. Now officials pressured the Indians to organize a business committee, whose members were to be tribally elected. Promises of economic aid and self-determination followed, but the hopes of Arapaho leaders were soon dashed because aid was minimal. Agricultural output declined. At the same time the population increased, the result of a better health-care system. The middle-aged leaders who were elected to the business council with the old chiefs' support were not able to demonstrate success to their followers in improving living conditions. The Arapaho did succeed in getting equal representation with the Cheyenne on the council, although the Cheyenne still outnumbered the Arapaho by two to one.

Economic decline and the advent of World War II caused many Arapaho to move to urban areas where they could find employment. Many sold their land. By 1951, two-thirds of the Cheyenne and the Arapaho were landless, and most of the rest owned only small fractional shares of the land that had been allotted to their deceased ancestors. Those in urban areas often returned to attend dances in the countryside, where the Arapaho retained campgrounds on a few remaining allotments, but few could make a living residing permanently on Arapaho lands.

After the 1930s, Arapaho had to go to Wyoming to participate in the Offerings Lodge; there were no more elderly ritual authorities in Oklahoma. By the early 1960s, the Southern Arapaho had far more difficulty than the Northern division mobilizing tribal members to work for common goals, support tribal leaders, and participate in a tribal sharing network. ▲

Therin Dewey, Jr., of Arapahoe on Wind River Reservation,
receives a diploma for graduating from the Head Start program.

THE NEW GENERATION: NORTHERN AND SOUTHERN ARAPAHO TODAY

In the 1960s public attitudes and government policies toward minorities changed. The struggles of civil rights activists to overcome discriminatory laws and customs led to greater tolerance for, and increased aid to, minority groups throughout the country. During the administrations of Presidents John Kennedy and Lyndon Johnson, legislative programs known respectively as the New Frontier and the Great Society provided government financing for a variety of social programs. These included civil rights enforcement, an increase in educational opportunities, housing, job training, and economic development.

Indian reservations and communities were eligible for a number of these programs. As a result, the role of tribal governments expanded as their officials acquired new responsibilities and power. Tribal officials were involved in administering housing, public works, education, and other War on Poverty projects initiated by the Johnson admin-

istration. In 1965, for example, the Department of Housing and Urban Development began an extensive program of building homes in Indian communities, and the Indian Health Service (a division of the Public Health Service) supported improvements in water supply and sanitation. The Elementary and Secondary Education Act of 1965 funded special programs for Indian students to increase their knowledge and appreciation of their cultural heritage.

Federal policy toward Indians in the 1970s centered on giving the tribal governments increased responsibility for administering government-funded programs. The Indian Self-Determination and Educational Assistance Act of 1975 provided a means by which tribes could contract with the federal government to manage programs that had formerly been run by federal officials.

During the 1980s the federal government did less for Indians; budget cuts terminated many government-related jobs and drastically reduced medical and other services to the needy. A general decline in oil prices also hurt the local economies of Wind River and Oklahoma. For the Northern Arapaho, the reservation and the community's commitment to helping one another were cushions against the economic reversals. The Southern Arapaho, who were living in non-Indian communities throughout western Oklahoma, had less to fall back on.

Today some extended Southern Arapaho families still live on inherited allotments in the Oklahoma countryside, but many more are clustered in tribal housing projects in Geary or in private homes in Canton. At least half of the Southern Arapaho, however, live outside the area that was originally allotted to the Arapaho. Very little land is still owned by the tribe—only about 75,000 acres out of the half-million allotted in 1891. Many older Arapaho own shares in the allotments of ancestors, and they receive a percentage of rental fees and royalties for oil and gas produced on their land. This income is small and unequally distributed among the population, but it allows elderly people to continue making an important economic contribution to the subsistence of their households.

As subagencies and the government boarding schools closed from the late 1920s through the 1970s, the lands on which they were situated, some 10,000 acres, reverted to the tribes. This tribally held property is leased for farming, grazing, and mineral development. Income from farming and grazing

leases—about $130,000 a year—pays for the tribal government's operating expenses and supports some programs to alleviate the poverty of tribal members. Most of the oil and gas royalties from the tribally owned land are distributed on a per-person basis once a year to the members of the Southern Cheyenne and the Southern Arapaho tribes. The payment is a small one.

Most of the Oklahoma Arapaho live in poverty. Unemployment in recent years has ranged from 40 to 70 percent (compared with a national unemployment rate of from 5 to 15 percent). There are not enough jobs locally, and Indians often face discrimination when they apply for jobs in the non-Indian world. Families get some income from employment and services subsidized by the federal government, which has contracted with the tribal government to operate programs such as Child Welfare and Indian Health. Many tribal members receive additional income in the form of public assistance, social security, or military pensions directly from state and federal sources.

Today the Southern Arapaho communities in the Geary and Canton areas each elect two members to represent them on the Cheyenne-Arapaho Business Committee. Four other elected members represent the four Cheyenne communities. Tribal members who live outside the Geary and Canton communities can be very influential in these elections and can also be candidates for these positions. Ballots are mailed to all enrolled tribal members, that is, all

The 1988 Cheyenne-Arapaho Business Committee. Front row, from left: *Arleen Kauley; Edward Heap of Birds, secretary; Juanita Learned, chairwoman; Alton Harrison, vice-chairman.* Back row, from left: *Jonathan Burgess; George Sutton; Floyd Black Bear; Viola Hatch, treasurer. The mural on the wall behind them, painted by Cheyenne artist, depicts elements of the peyote ceremony.*

those who have applied for tribal membership and been judged by the tribal council as having sufficient Indian ancestry to qualify. Since 1966, women have been elected to the committee. Members, who receive salaries, oversee federally funded programs and serve as advocates for the people in their relations with oil companies, local and state officials, and the federal government. Recently, they have instituted three tribally owned businesses, including a bingo operation at Concho, site of the tribal offices. The committee's job is particularly difficult because its constituency includes nonreservation Indians whose situation differs from that of res-

ervation residents. Nonreservation Indians receive fewer federal services than those on reservations and, because they live in the midst of the mainstream culture, experience extensive discrimination.

Business committee members are generally middle-aged. Elders continue to be respected, but those in Oklahoma have less influence than their Northern Arapaho counterparts because the center of Arapaho religious ritual is in Wyoming. Young people, on the other hand, have greater independence than they formerly did. Many young men and women today earn college degrees and then attempt to obtain jobs work-

Southern Arapaho children near their school in Canton, Oklahoma, in 1986.

ing for the tribes in managerial positions; others choose to seek wage work in urban areas throughout Oklahoma or elsewhere. The children now attend public schools, where they are a minority. They learn their place in Arapaho society through family life and by participating in benefit dances and other community activities.

Life in the Geary and Canton Arapaho communities revolves, to a great extent, around the benefit dances. These are held almost every weekend. Arapaho living elsewhere often return to attend the dances, which raise money for many causes, from helping needy individuals to aiding service clubs to covering the expenses of summer powwows, or gatherings.

A dance is usually sponsored by a family or an organization. Planning for a benefit dance begins many weeks in advance. The sponsor first chooses at least seven people to serve as head staff—a head singer, head male and female dancers, young boy and girl dancers, a master of ceremonies, and an arena director. The head singer is responsible for gathering a drum group together to sing at the dance. Head dancers lead the dancing and urge others to join in. The master of ceremonies presides over the event, often choosing the songs and deciding on the sequence in which they will be performed. Finally, the arena director makes sure the hall or grounds where the dance will be held are ready, and helps carry the food and gifts exchanged at the dance. These positions are modern counterparts of older ones; the master of ceremonies, for example, is equivalent to the camp crier of earlier days who announced to the people the consensus-based decisions of the elders.

The entire family of every member of the head staff is expected to help collect the gifts and food that will be given away at the dance. The sponsor arranges for food to be cooked and also obtains gifts for the giveaway, which is held before the main events of the dance begin. Every person on the head staff give gifts to each of the others, so several hours are needed for all the gifts to be presented. The head singer, for example, gives at least a blanket to each of the other men, a shawl to each of the women, and a basket of groceries to each of the children on the head staff. After the gifts are presented, a special dance honors the sponsoring family

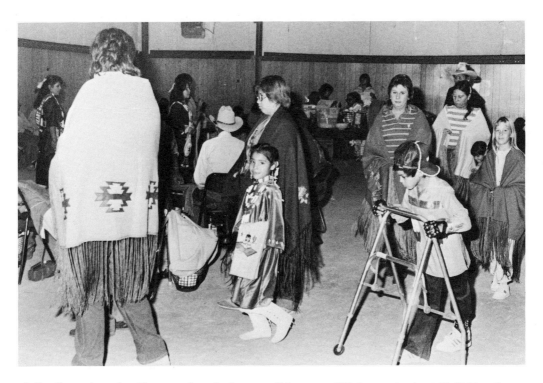

A Southern Arapaho-Cheyenne benefit dance at Watonga, Oklahoma, in the mid-1980s. On the table are baskets of groceries to be raffled off to raise money or to be given to members of the head staff of the dance.

that gave gifts. The people in attendance join in the dance and then contribute money to the sponsoring family, which donates the money to the evening's cause. Gift exchanges help to maintain the sense of mutual obligation and goodwill that are essential to the continuation of these rituals. During the dance the master of ceremonies can call for dances to honor a category of people, such as veterans or people from a particular area; members of the category so honored are then obligated to dance and also contribute money to the evening's cause.

Most Southern Arapaho families become involved as sponsors or head staff members in at least one benefit dance a year. Leaders, such as elected officials, and people who are employed, especially those who work for the tribe, are expected to participate frequently.

Some of the money raised in benefit dances goes to sponsor summer powwows, for which tribal members may travel hundreds of miles to attend. The Geary Arapaho sponsor a powwow in July, and the Canton Arapaho hold one in August. These are followed by an even larger powwow in September sponsored by both the Southern Arapaho and the Southern Cheyenne.

At the powwows, veterans, various leaders, and elders are recognized and honored by the community. Noted dancers from many different tribes enter contests and compete for cash prizes. Because dances were once forbidden, their persistence today symbolizes to the Arapaho their success in resisting exploitation and victimization by the federal government and non-Indians. The survival and contemporary elaboration of the dancing tradition is perceived as a hard-won victory.

Peyote ceremonies continue to be a focus of spiritual life, drawing together not only Arapaho from Geary and Canton but also those living outside the area of the former reservation. Participants may vow to sponsor (that is, pay the expenses of) a peyote ceremony as a prayer-sacrifice. Today the peyote religion is known as the Native American Church. The supernatural help sought may be in the form of a cure, a child's health and success in life, or other similar entreaties. Many Arapaho also attend Christian churches, primarily of Protestant faiths. But the most important ritual for many Arapaho remains the Offering Lodge, held every summer at Wind River in Wyoming. Many Southern Arapaho travel there regularly to participate in this ceremony held by the Northern Arapaho. Some of the money raised through benefit dances during the year is used to pay for expenses and ritual obligations. In recent years, an increasing number of

Southern Arapaho have been going to Wyoming to celebrate the Offerings Lodge. Like powwows, the Offerings Lodge brings all Arapaho together to express their commitment to the Arapaho community and identity.

Although the two divisions visit, communicate, and share the Arapaho identity, they continue to have different experiences. The 4,000 Northern Arapaho are still centered on Wind River Reservation, living largely on their allotments. In the mid-1960s most of them were living in mobile homes or small log or frame houses, often without plumbing and electricity. Since then, new or remodeled frame or prefabricated homes, ranch style or split-level, have been built on most of the allotments, and there are two housing projects, all built through federally funded programs.

Wind River Reservation is 55 miles long and 70 miles wide—largely wide-open space. Very few non-Indians reside on the reservation, and those that do have little contact with the Indians. The Arapaho do their shopping in the two Wyoming towns, Lander and Riverton, that border the reservation but have little personal contact with the residents of the towns.

Northern Arapaho children still grow up in extended family settlements. These consist of several houses clustered together, with the grandparents' household at the spiritual and social center. Because parents often work, grandparents or older siblings usually watch the small children during the day. Adults accept responsibility for caring for the children of their brothers and sisters. Children have many grandparents, because they call the brothers and sisters of their grandparents by the same terms as they use for their actual grandmother and grandfather. Children may live for a time in the household of one relative, then in that of another. When old enough to help elders, children may live with their grandparents. Thus child care is widely diffused. Children learn to be unobtrusive in their relations with others, to repress anger, to defer to elders, to be generous with possessions, and to persuade rather than demand.

During the summer children ride the family's horses and play with their cousins—whom they know as "brothers" and "sisters." They attend public school on the reservation during the remainder of the year. Few non-Indian children attend these schools, and Arapaho parents have great influence over school policies. Arapaho language and culture, particularly handcrafts, are taught there. In 1972 and 1976 two high schools were contracted for by organized groups of parents with the federal government so that Arapaho children could complete secondary school on the reservation in an environment that affirmed tribal values.

For teenagers, sports are a major preoccupation and a source of community pride; Indian high school teams play, often quite successfully, against their counterparts from Wyoming's non-Indian communities. After they graduate from high school, some young men now go on to college, while many join the armed services or seek employment on the reservation. But there are not enough jobs on the reservation, in part because of cuts in spending on federal programs in the 1980s. After young women graduate from high school they also go to college or seek employment.

Dave Bell, who helped the Wyoming Indian High School Chiefs become the state champions in 1988. School teams are a source of pride for the Northern Arapaho of Wind River.

Until a young man reaches his thirties, he is considered not yet stable or settled and has only a limited role in community activities. Young men do join some clubs, sometimes in the capacity of helpers or apprentices. Girls assist their mothers in their club activities. Young men and women increasingly marry while still in their teens, even before they have found employment. Today some newly married couples live in housing projects, but they still spend much of their time at their parents' and grandparents' homes.

Mature men and women attempt to find work on the reservation. Most job openings are on tribal government projects, but these are limited. Even at the peak of President Johnson's War on Poverty programs, unemployment among the Wind River Arapaho was 48 percent. Those who do have jobs help support relatives who are unemployed. Outside of work, much time is spent helping with activities of the clubs, such as the Christmas and Memorial clubs, and those who aspire to leadership positions in the community are particu-

American Legion members at Wind River lead the grand entry parade at a community powwow. The young women with numbers on their costumes will participate in a dance contest.

larly diligent about donating time and money.

Every fall the local American Legion posts and associated Women's Auxiliaries sponsor a Veterans' Day dance. These two posts, located on the reservation in the areas of Ethete and Arapahoe, are composed primarily of Arapaho veterans of World War II, although younger veterans sometimes join in as well. They also conduct flag ceremonies at events throughout the year and organize military funerals. In the winter, the Christmas Club sponsors a week of dancing and other activities. The Memorial Club assumes responsibility for a yearly spring dance and for maintaining and decorating graves. Two committees organize the summer powwows that are attended by tribes from all over the Plains. People come to camp, visit, and participate in games and dance contests at the two powwows. Women have an important role in all these events; they not only prepare the food for communal feasts but are also responsible for giveaway ceremonies. At powwow giveaways, families honor various relatives by giving away property (such as quilts, shawls, kitchen utensils, and clothing) to others.

An elected six-member business council works with the Shoshone Business Council to manage Wind River's lands and resources. The council decides on those who can lease tribal land, giving preference to Indians, and purchases land from individuals who wish to sell their allotments. Most reserva-

Elder Clina Willow teaches the hand game, a traditional guessing game, to students at Wyoming Indian High School.

tion land is still held in trust; 78 percent is tribally owned, and most of the remainder of the reservation's almost 2½ million acres is owned by individual Arapaho. Recently, the Northern Arapaho business council instituted several tribally owned businesses, including a gas station and two grocery stores; the tribe has also owned a cattle ranch since 1940.

In the late 1970s, oil and gas royalties and bonuses from tribal lands brought the Northern Arapaho $4.5 million each year. Eighty-five percent of this was distributed in per-person pay-

State and local officials look over a scale model for a new Wyoming Indian High School building, following groundbreaking ceremonies for the project in April 1988. At left is W. Patrick Goggles, an Arapaho who is chairman of the school's board of trustees.

ments; out of the remainder, the business council was given a budget of about $400,000 to administer, in addition to monies received from federal programs. It uses some of this money, plus loans from the federal government, to buy—and thus keep in the tribe—land from individual Arapaho who wish to sell their allotments.

Much of the Northern Arapaho's budget supports the activities of the clubs and pays for essentials—such as groceries, necessary travel, school supplies, and funeral costs—for needy individuals. The council also gives hiring preference to those who are most in need. The council seeks to pressure the federal government into assuming greater financial responsibility for the reservation. Its members believe that financial support is a federal obligation resulting from the treaty relationship between the Northern Arapaho and the U.S. government.

Northern Arapaho political life still depends on reaching a consensus. Elders are particularly influential in setting group goals and mobilizing community support for those goals. Elders also mobilize support for the members of the business council, who in turn call a meeting of the entire tribe to discuss particularly important issues. The council's members receive no salary but are paid a per-day fee each time they meet. In the late 1960s, 1970s and 1980s, no women served on the council. (Generally the Arapaho view public advocacy as more suitable for men than women.) Every two years the Northern Arapaho also elect an Entertainment Committee whose six members coordinate and supervise community celebrations and oversee the spending of money allocated to clubs. The members of both the business council and entertainment committee are generally leaders in secular concerns, whereas elders retain authority in religious matters.

A group of elderly men and women supervises sacred ceremonies at Wind River. One of these ritual leaders takes care of the Sacred Pipe and presides over its rites. The Pipe contains, and reminds the Arapaho of, the supernatural power available to them if they as a tribal group continue to cooperate with one another, act in harmony, and fulfill their ritual responsibilities.

The most important religious ceremony involving the entire community is the Offerings Lodge. In July all Northern Arapaho families—and many Southern Arapaho families—camp for seven days at Wind River. Individuals who have vowed to do so make the prayer-sacrifice in the lodge. The participants' families prepare food that is exchanged throughout the entire camp, thus symbolizing tribal unity. Everyone attempts to concentrate on the sacred occasion and avoid any social conflict. In the lodge, the story of creation is dramatized, and participants, old and young, male and female, fulfill their vows to the Creator through prayer and fasting. In recent years the Arapaho have devoted an increasing amount of money and effort to this ceremony. Many Indians from other tribes travel hundreds of miles to be present at the event.

The Offerings Lodge, like the language, values, and other aspects of Northern Arapaho life that the non-Indian society once tried to eradicate, has endured. Today it remains a source of strength and fulfillment for the Arapaho people of Oklahoma as well as those of Wyoming. ▲

BIBLIOGRAPHY

Annual Reports of the Commissioner of Indian Affairs. Washington, D.C.: Government Printing Office, 1846–1904.

Bass, Althea. *The Arapaho Way: a Memoir of an Indian Boyhood.* New York: Potter, 1966.

Berthrong, Donald J. *The Cheyenne and Arapaho Ordeal: Reservation and Agency Life in the Indian Territory.* Norman: University of Oklahoma Press, 1976.

————. "Legacies of the Dawes Act: Bureaucrats and Land Thieves at the Cheyenne-Arapaho Agencies of Oklahoma." In *Arizona and the West.* (Winter 1975): 335–54.

Dorsey, George A. *The Arapaho Sun Dance.* Field Columbian Museum Anthropological Series 4, 1903.

Dorsey, George A., and Alfred L. Kroeber. *Traditions of the Arapaho.* Field Columbian Museum Anthropological Series 5, 1903.

Fowler, Loretta. *Arapahoe Politics, 1851–1978: Symbols in Crises of Authority.* Lincoln: University of Nebraska Press, 1982.

————. *Shared Symbols, Contested Meanings: Gros Ventre Culture and History, 1778–1984.* Ithaca: Cornell University Press, 1987.

Hafen, LeRoy R., ed. *Pike's Peak Gold Rush Guidebooks of 1859.* Glendale: Arthur H. Clark, 1941.

Hilger, M. Inez. *Arapahoe Child Life and Its Cultural Background.* Bureau of American Ethnology Bulletin 148. Washington, D.C.: Government Printing Office, 1952.

Kroeber, Alfred L. *The Arapaho.* American Museum of Natural History Bulletin 18, 1902.

Michelson, Truman. "Narrative of an Arapaho Woman." *American Anthropologist,* N.S., 35, 1933: 595–610.

Salzmann, Zdenek. *The Arapaho Indians: A Research Guide and Bibliography.* New York: Greenwood Press, 1988.

Seger, John H., and Stanley Vestal, eds. *Early Days Among the Cheyenne and Arapaho Indians.* Norman: University of Oklahoma Press, 1956.

THE ARAPAHO AT A GLANCE

TRIBE   *Arapaho*

CULTURE AREA   *Great Plains*

GEOGRAPHY   *at contact, the northern Plains; from the mid-19th century, Northern Arapaho on the plains of southern Wyoming and northern Colorado; southern Arapaho on the plains of west-central Oklahoma and southern Kansas*

LINGUISTIC FAMILY   *Algonquian*

CURRENT POPULATION   *approximately 7,000*

FIRST CONTACT   *Jean Baptiste Trudeau, French, 1795*

FEDERAL STATUS   *recognized; Wind River Reservation in Wyoming is the Northern Arapaho tribal land; Southern Arapaho have no reservation.*

GLOSSARY

agent A person appointed by the Bureau of Indian Affairs to supervise U.S. government programs on a reservation and/or in a specific region. After 1908 the title superintendent replaced agent.

Algonquian language family A group of languages, spoken by Indian peoples of northeastern America, the Great Lakes, and the Plains, that have similar grammatical and pronunciation patterns and related vocabulary. Algonquian-speaking tribes include the Arapaho, Cheyenne, Narragansett, and Abenaki.

allotment U.S. policy, first applied in 1887, to break up tribally owned reservations by assigning individual farms and ranches to Indians. Intended as much to discourage traditional communal activities as to encourage private farming and assimilate Indians into mainstream American life.

artifact Any object made by human beings, such as a tool, garment, dwelling, or ornament; also, any marking in or on the earth indicating the previous existence of such an object.

assimilation Adoption by individuals of the customs of another, usually dominant, society; a means by which the host society recruits new members and replaces a subordinate society's culture. The United States, as well as most American Indian societies, gained new members in this manner.

band A loosely organized group of people who live in one area and are bound together by the need for food and defense, by family ties, or by other common attributes.

breech cloth or **breechclout** A soft piece of hide or cloth, usually worn by American Indian men, wrapped between the legs and held in place by a belt or string around the waist.

Bureau of Indian Affairs (BIA) A U.S. government agency within the Department of the Interior. Originally intended to manage trade and other relations with Indians, the BIA now seeks to develop and implement programs that encourage Indians to manage their own affairs and to improve their educational opportunities and general social and economic well-being.

civilization program U.S. policy of the late 19th and early 20th centuries designed to change the Indians' way of life so that it resembled that of non-Indians. These programs usually focused on converting Indians to Christianity and encouraging them to become farmers.

fee patent The right to hold land as personal property, without restriction; land ownership.

Ghost Dance movement A religious and cultural revival movement that spread among Indians in the 1890s and centered on the belief that non-Indian newcomers would disappear and the Indians' traditional world would return if certain rituals were performed. Among some tribes, these rituals included dances that were performed for days at a time.

giveaway A ceremony practiced by many Plains Indian tribes in which members of a family, represented principally by women, publicly distribute property to others in honor of a relative, to express their appreciation for receiving an honor, or to acknowledge the acceptance of a responsibility. Non-Indian federal officials and missionaries objected to giveaways because they undermined adjustment to practices of free enterprise and personal saving.

gold rush A large-scale migration, beginning in 1849, from the eastern United States to the goldfields of California. The major traveling routes of the gold rush crossed the territories of many Plains Indian peoples, including the Arapaho.

Great Plains A flat, dry region in central North America, primarily covered by lush grasslands.

horticulture Food production using human muscle power and simple hand tools to plant and harvest domesticated crops.

Indian Claims Commission (ICC) A U.S. government body, created by an act of Congress in 1946, to hear and rule on claims brought by Indians against the United States for unfulfilled treaty terms such as nonpayment.

Indian New Deal Program inaugurated by the Indian Reorganization Act of 1934, designed to remove government restrictions on Indian traditions and to encourage autonomous development of Indian communities.

Indian Reorganization Act (IRA) The 1934 federal law that ended the policy of allotting plots of land to individuals and encouraged the political and economic development of reservation communities. The act also provided for the creation of autonomous tribal governments.

irrigation The routing of water to dry land through ditches, canals, or other means in order to make cultivation possible.

medicine power The ability to accomplish particular ends, such as feats of bravery in war or curing of illnesses, by invoking and controlling spiritual powers.

Offerings Lodge An Arapaho religious ceremony whose participants have vowed to sacrifice through prayer, fasting, and other means in return for supernatural aid, and whose ceremonies dramatize events of creation.

oral tradition The practice of preserving and passing on tribal history and mythology through the telling of memorized or learned stories.

peyote A button or growth of the Lophophora cactus, native to Texas and the northern Mexican states, that is used as the vehicle, or channel, for prayer in several American Indian religious practices.

polygyny A society's marriage custom in which a man may have more than one wife; a man's wives are often members of the same family, usually sisters.

powwow An Indian social gathering thàt includes feasting, dancing, rituals, and arts and crafts displays, to which other Indian groups as well as non-Indians are now often invited.

Quakers The familiar name for members of the Religious Society of Friends, a mystical and pacifist group founded in England by George Fox in the 17th century. Quakers were active in efforts to help Indians during the 19th century.

reservation or *reserve* A tract of land set aside by treaty for Indian occupation and use.

Sun Dance A name non-Indians gave to the Offerings Lodge and similar rituals of other tribes.

tribe A society consisting of several or many separate communities united by kinship, culture, language, and such other social factors as clans, religious organizations, and economic and political institutions. A federally and/or state recognized "tribe," such as the Southern or the Northern Arapaho, is usually a land-owning, corporate group with its own government.

trust The relationship between the federal government and many Indian tribes, dating from the late 19th century. Government agents managed Indians' business dealings, including land transactions and rights to natural resources, because the Indians were considered legally incompetent to manage their own affairs.

vision guest A fast and vigil undertaken by Indian individuals (usually males but occasionally females as well) in the hope of receiving a sign from a supernatural power who might guide and protect the vision seeker through life. The vigil usually required extended solitude and fasting outdoors at a distance from the community.

PICTURE CREDITS

LORETTA FOWLER is professor of anthropology at City College of the City University of New York. She holds a B.A. from Smith College and a Ph.D. from the University of Illinois. She has been a fellow of the Smithsonian Institution and the D'Arcy McNickle Center for the History of the American Indian at the Newberry Library. She is the author of several articles and books on Plains Indians, including *Arapahoe Politics, 1851–1978: Symbols in Crises of Authority* (1982) and *Shared Symbols, Contested Meanings: Gros Ventre Culture and History, 1778–1984* (1987).

FRANK W. PORTER III, general editor of INDIANS OF NORTH AMERICA, is director of the Chelsea House Foundation for American Indian Studies. He holds a B.A., M.A., and Ph.D. from the University of Maryland. He has done extensive research concerning the Indians of Maryland and Delaware and is the author of numerous articles on their history, archaeology, geography, and ethnography. He was formerly director of the Maryland Commission on Indian Affairs and American Indian Research and Resource Institute, Gettysburg, Pennsylvania, and he has received grants from the Delaware Humanities Forum, the Maryland Committee for the Humanities, the Ford Foundation, and the National Endowment for the Humanities, among others. Dr. Porter is the author of *The Bureau of Indian Affairs* in the Chelsea House KNOW YOUR GOVERNMENT series.